The Firefighting Buff's Guide To New York City

The Firefighting Buff's Guide To New York City

The Five Borough, Five Alarm Reference To The Second Homes of New York's Bravest

Come out, Buy a Metrocard, and see Rescue 4, Ladder 79, and Engine 240 too!

By Joseph Natale Schneiderman

WRITERS CLUB PRESS
San Jose New York Lincoln Shanghai

The Firefighting Buff's Guide To New York City
The Five Borough, Five Alarm Reference To The Second Homes of New York's Bravest

Writers Club Press
an imprint of iUniverse, Inc.

For information address:
iUniverse, Inc.
5220 S. 16th St., Suite 200
Lincoln, NE 68512
www.iuniverse.com

ISBN: 0-595-24602-8

Printed in the United States of America

I dedicate this book to the 1117 firefighters of the Fire Department of the City of New York who have made the supreme sacrifice in the discharge of their duty protecting life and property in the City of New York, and their families, and in particular the 343 on Sept. 11th who responded to boxes 8087 (the north tower) and 9999 (the south tower) at the World Trade Center; who rushed into the 110 stories of hell when others rushed out. I also dedicate it to the 60 police officers from the City of New York and the Port Authority of New York and New Jersey who also rushed in when others rushed out, and never came home, and to all the rescuers who died at the World Trade Center on that summer day when the world changed. I also dedicate this work to my loving father and mother, who have always supported me. I would also like to dedicate this book to a few people who have always supported my interest in firefighting despite my overly repetitive discussion of it. It would take too long to name names, so you all know who you are. Finally, I dedicate this book to all the brothers in battle currently in the FDNY, all 11,000 of you. You are a large part of the inspiration for this book! Thank you all!

Contents

INTRODUCTION

Being a firefighting buff myself, I always wished there was a book with detailed information on firehouses in New York City. Well, my dad and I together have been to 43 firehouses in New York City, and both of us carry a deep passion for it. My dad, although not quite the buff I am, has had his share of interest in firefighting. It began when he was in art school when he was just a bit younger than I am now, on 57th Street in Midtown. He drew a wonderful picture of the beautiful firehouse on West 58th Street in Manhattan (due north of his art school), Engine Company 23, and also drew sketches of two of the heroes of the infamous 23rd Street fire. That was 1966—1967, when he was not yet 16. His interest then lay dormant for about 25 years. But during those 25 years, he earned a degree in the classics from Yale, went to Tufts Medical School, got married, and had a son, me.

From an early age, I was interested in firefighting and knew I wanted to be a firefighter. My dad believed it was fitting for the age, as most 3 and 4 year olds are interested in firemen. But as the years progressed, he realized I was serious. I really wanted to be a firefighter and save lives. I still want to be a firefighter, now more than ever. But during those years, between 1992 roughly and 1995, we visited 97 firehouses, including 64 in 1992.

We visited mainly local fire houses in the Farmington Valley and Winsted area in Connecticut, but we visited our fair share in New York City, particularly the Bronx around Pelham Bay Park. In 1992, we visited 13 firehouses in New York City, 8 in the Bronx alone. We learned about our firehouses either through chances of fate or the *AIA Guide to New York City*. In particular, there was one on Great Jones Street that we found out about in the AIA guide that we both took a liking to, Engine Company 33, Ladder Company 9. But we didn't find out that it was Ladder 9 until 1996. I also learned about Engine Company 54, Ladder Company 4, and Battalion 9 on 8th Avenue, and really wanted to visit. I also learned about Engine Company 154 on Staten Island, and wanted to visit them for the same reason as Engine 54, just because. It's a kid thing. I guess one reason is because I liked the number "54". I also had learned about Engine Company 4 and Ladder Company 15's old house on Water Street in downtown Manhattan which had been destroyed and wanted to visit them. I guess the reason there is because 4 is my lucky number.

From 1992 to 1997, we visited 24 firehouses in New York City. That is more than half of our 43 visited together. Just recently I visited twelve additional ones without him, but he didn't mind at all. We had many fun times. We also visited at least two out-of-service firehouses, the former Engine Company 31 on Lafayette Street in Manhattan and the former Ladder Company 118 or Brooklyn Fire Headquarters, which is the famous Jay Street Firehouse. So before we begin, I want all of you to extend your heartfelt thanks to my wonderful father, Henry Schneiderman, M.D..

Additionally, I would like you thank my mother, Rosemaria Memoli Schneiderman, who inspired me to write this book and helped me turn a computer database of firehouses (how I keep track of all my visits, New York City or otherwise) turn into this reality. Mom, thanks for all the support and ideas. Also Mom, thank you for having me include "The Ten House" on Liberty Street. Also, I would like you to thank my English teacher during my sophomore year of high school, Ms. Kristina Stahl, who taught me more about writing and the propriety of it in sophomore year than in all my previous years of school, and probably without her teaching, this book would be a disorganized, disoriented excuse for a book. Ms. Stahl, thanks for everything!

Finally, I would like you to thank my best friend of the past 7 years, Mike Ulloa, who helped me scan in the images you will see (and have already seen!) in this book! Also Mike, thank you for checking on "Kevin Kane Place" and "Alfred Ronaldson Place" in Brooklyn and the Bronx (we'll talk about them later). Mike, thanks for your technology and time, and hopefully, we'll all see you at Broadway and 50th in a couple of years! Finally (this is the last time, really), I would also like to thank Michael Loughrin from the FDNY Public Relations office and a kind firefighter named Joe from Engine 236 in East New York, Brooklyn (working the PR office that day) who took some time out of their schedules to take a look at this book about their profession. Mr. Loughrin, thank you, and Joe, I'll see ya at 236 Engine soon (with luck)!

Well, let's get going. First of all, the term for going to firehouses is buffing. I will further explain buffing in Chapter 2. So keep that in mind. Before we begin, I need you to complete a small quiz. Don't worry, it's not one that requires studying. It's just one that you already know the answers to, because they are all in your head! Good luck and enjoy!

Joseph N. Schneiderman

March 21, 2002 and July 19, 2002

To contact the author, please send e-mail to

jstaten121@aol.com

1

THE QUIZ

This quiz is incredibly easy to take. Please choose a letter that best answers the question, much like the SAT or a multiple choice test. Good luck!!

1. **So, What do you think of New York City?**

   a. Like Homer Simpson, I think it is a hellhole and will never go.

   b. After Sept. 11th, I don't think I wanna go. I am sad about the 3,000 deaths.

   c. I love the city, everything, I just wish I didn't live in Idaho or Kentucky.

   d. I have family from the city, my mother and father. One of my family members actually worked for the city, and I love everything, from City Hall down to the Rats!!

2. **What do you think of the FDNY?**

   a. They are a bunch of uneducated hose jockeys. Disgusting!

   b. After Sept. 11th, they are depressed and overworked, good men and women. I am sad about the deaths of their 343 comrades.

    c.   I think it is a noble, honorable, and wonderful organization, and I enjoy learning about it, but I don't have the time to pay my respects.

    d.   I love it, wanna be a part of it, spend way too much time thinking about it, have pictures of fire engines on my computer, and know firefighters by name.

3.   **How much do you know about the FDNY?**

    a.   They drive oversized, polluting red boxes of trucks. What else is there to know?!?

    b.   After Sept. 11th, too much about the deaths of firemen. I wish they could have peace.

    c.   I have read *Report from Engine Company 82* and enjoyed it in my limited spare time, I also know of some firehouses here and there in Manhattan, but want to learn more.

    d.   I have been to 30 or more firehouses and know that the organization dates back to the 1660's, the paid fire department began in 1865, there is no Battalion 5 or Engine 2, 1972 was a terrible year when many companies were disbanded, Mack CFs have become icons of the Fire Department, I own shirts from all 5 boroughs, I know the story of Rescue 1's quarters (you know, that story),I have read *Report from Engine Company 82* and want to spread knowledge about it, and I know that on Oct. 17th, 1966, 12 firemen died, several from Ladder 7 on East 29th Street, and for my dad's 50th Birthday, I compiled a list of all the firehouses we had visited and as a combined 50th Birthday/ Hanukkah/Christmas present, I bought him an FDNY Chief's hat (not the helmet the chiefs use).

4.   **How many Rescue companies have you visited?**

    a.   None, they don't rescue anything!

b. After Sept.11th, none. I think after all the deaths, the men, women and companies are too scarred.

c. Rescue 1 only, walking back from the *U.S.S. Intrepid.*

d. 3 or more Rescue Companies, Rescue 1 and two from the outer boroughs, know the locations of all the Rescue companies, know of at least two firefighters by name who died in Sept. 11th, and own patches from at least 2 Rescue Companies and shirts from at least 3 Rescue Companies.

5. **How many firehouses do you want to visit?**

a. None! Don't you get it, I got this book by accident instead of a Britney Spears CD and hate it!

b. After Sept. 11th, I'm not sure I want to visit any. I don't know how well the firefighters will react.

c. At least two, but I'm not sure I'll have the time.

d. All of the remaining ones I haven't visited, including Squad 288/Haz-Mat 1,Engine 308/Battalion 51/JFK Hose Wagon, Engine 324/Satellite 4/Division 14, Engine 285/Ladder 142 and Squad 270/Division 13 in Queens, Ladder 18/Battalion 4, Engine 16/Ladder 7, and Engine 65 in Manhattan, Engine 151/ Ladder 76, Engine 152/Battalion 21, Engine 157/Ladder 80, Engine 159/Satellite 5 and Marine 9 on Staten Island, Engine 82/ Ladder 31, Engine 60/Ladder 17/Battalion 14, Engine 75/ Ladder 33/Battalion 19, Rescue 3/Collapse Rescue Unit and Engine 68/Ladder 49 in the Bronx, Engine 212/Hi-Ex Foam 212, Engine 231/Ladder 120/Battalion 44, Squad 1, and Rescue 2 in Brooklyn.

6. **What music should you listen to while buffing (not while at the firehouse of course)?**

a. You don't get it, do you? I hate firehouses and firemen and love Britney Spears!

b. After Sept. 11th, patriotic music, but I'm not sure.

c. All the music I like, whatever it is, if I could go buffing.

d. Meatloaf, Phil Collins, Bruce Springsteen, the "Buffy the Vampire Slayer Musical", basically, all 260 songs and soundbits that your author has, in particular "Everything Louder than Everything Else", and "In the Air Tonight", "Good Girls Go To Heaven", "Bat Out of Hell", "Don't Lose My Number", "One More Night", "Homer Drunk", "Homer Peeing", "Moviephone", "George's Answering Machine", "Take Me Home", "Atlantic City", "Born in the U.S.A.", "Tenth Avenue Freezeout", "I Will Walk Through the Fire"(from the Buffy the Vampire Slayer Musical), "Tubthumping", "Modern Girl", "I Would Do Anything For Love (But I Won't Do That)" and "Redneck Christmas."

7. **How many model fire engines do you own or wish to own?**

a. None! I hate firemen, firefighting, the color red, and everything that has to do with firemen, I dwell instead on Britney Spears 24/7/365 and could care less.

b. After Sept. 11th, just one, on my dashboard, but I think it broke when I took that speed bump at 80 mph.

c. I have one solo Engine from Manhattan, but my spare time and money is limited, so I can't buy any more.

d. I own an Engine from Morningside Heights and want to buy the Engine 82/Ladder 31 set, and want to buy Engine 46 and Rescue 3.

8. **How often do you take photos of firehouses?**

a. NONE! You really don't get it, do you, you obsessed idiot, I hate you, I hate the world, and like I'd never want to see a firehouse, ever.

b.   After Sept. 11th, I'm not sure I want to take photos of fire-houses, all those black flags are depressing.

c.   In my limited spare time, photos of every one I can.

d.   I dream about it, take at least one photo per month, visit at least one firehouse per month, and have several albums full. I grab firehouse photos even on non-formal buffing outings.

9.   **Do you try to get your family into buffing?**

a.   Stop your damn tirade! I hate firehouses, and could care less about the City of New York!

b.   After Sept. 11th, their feelings are way too frayed.

c.   In my limited free time with them, always.

d.   My dad has accompanied me to 90% of the firehouses I've been to, my mom is into it in her own way, my uncle wants in, and I have friends who like it.

10. **How many _DISBANDED_ (not currently in service) fire companies can you name?**

a.   Look here, you freak of nature, I don't care! I like Britney Spears. MMMMMM Britney Spears.

b.   After Sept. 11th, who knows? So many of them lost men.

c.   Engine 2 and Engine 30 at least, but my limited spare time prevents me from knowing more.

d.   Engines 2, 11, 12, 13, 17, 19, 20, 25, 27, 29, 30, 31, 32, 49, 56, 77, 78, 85, 203, 208, 215, 232, 296, 333, Ladders 171,193, High Ladder 1, Squads 2, 3, 4,5, the Super Pumper, Searchlight 1, Salvage 1, Battalions 5, 24, 25, 34, 36,55,56,59, 60, Divisions 2, 4,9, 10,16, 17, Marines 2,5,7,8 and Tactical Control Unit (a fancy name for a ladder company assigned to handle runs during peak hours) 712 from *Report from Engine Company 82.*

Scoring:

For Every A, zero points.

For Every B, 10 points.

For Every C, 100 points.

For Every D, 1000 points.

Interpretation of Scoring:

Score of 10 or less—This book obviously is not for you. Continue whatever you're doing.

Score of 11 to 100—You really are depressed about Sept. 11th. You need some help.

Score of 100 to 1000—This book is perfect for you! You will need some spare time, but this book will make you a buff!

Score of more than 1000—Oh my Lord! Does cloning exist? You are one of three things—A former firefighter, me, or a really crazed buff! This book will help you too!

2

SO, WHAT IS BUFFING?

So, you've completed the quiz, and regardless of your score, you're still reading this book. Wonderful. Well, what is buffing? Since the dictionary doesn't list it, I'll give you my special Joseph definition. Buffing, according to the dictionary of Joseph, 2002 edition, is going to firehouses, at least 1, on one day, taking photos, and meeting firefighters. Sometimes, if you're lucky, you can meet their dogs and mascots, Dalmatians. In FDNY colloquial, buffing means volunteering at another company or firehouse for a shift.

Having been to 190 firehouses, I have learned a good deal about buffing, and thus have come up with some buffing etiquette. Although you may not think you need etiquette, you do. So, here are the **10 rules of buffing etiquette,** that go for New York City firehouses and firehouses in general, everywhere from the smallest volunteer firehouse in Eagle Bay,NY to the superstation in Baltimore.

THE 10 RULES OF BUFFING ETIQUETTE

If you are going buffing with someone who does not have equal interest, thank them for their time and energy that they are putting in, and try to make it up to them by buying them lunch or a snack or something thoughtful.

If you are buffing solo, keep your wits about you, and remember to keep in touch with someone.

Don't barge in. Wait to be invited into the firehouse, or ask to come in politely, explaining who you are.

A full tour of everything should not be expected, particularly in city firehouses.

At volunteer firehouses, remember to not take up too much time, as the volunteers have other work they may need to do.

The most welcome sign to go into a firehouse is open doors (the garage doors), but if nobody is around, respect the empty firehouse.

Always remember, if you meet a firefighter who gives you his or her name, to send a thank you note.

If you have a pre-arranged tour, make sure to express thanks before the tour begins.

If you see a black flag over a firehouse, remember to express condolences to the firefighters you meet over the loss of their comrades.

HAVE FUN AND TAKE LOTS OF PHOTOS!

Well, now that we've completed buffing etiquette, what's next? Oh yes!

Pictures!

Any camera works fine, but don't bring a tripod or too much accessories as it could be cumbersome, unless you are a real professional photographer. The best type of camera is a point-and-shoot, anything from a Funsaver to a Fuji. My recommendation is the Fuji 312 Discovery. It's my personal camera and it may sound biased coming from me, but it's the perfect camera for a buff. It can take panoramic shots, good for photographing entire fire engines. Remember to get your photos developed ASAP to share with any other buffs in your life!

What's next? Oh yes!

What to Eat

Well, eating 4 ounces of miso soup is not a good idea nor is eating 30 habanero buffalo wings. You want to eat nice,well balanced meals before and after your buffing, and have little snacks in between. A good eat is something like a big sandwich, or a burger, with some fruit for balance. You also want to drink juice and water, and not alcohol.

Getting Around NYC

One last issue before we begin. Use the subway and buses. Make sure you have bought a Metrocard, as that will help you quite a bit. Metrocards are refillable, and you can buy dollar amounts from $3 to $80 or one-day passes for unlimited rides (a big fat bargain!). Scout out subway lines to your firehouses, scout out buses, everything! Check out some subway hubs too, like Fulton Street in Lower Manhattan, Union Square, Times Square, Penn Station, Columbus Circle, and Court Street-Borough Hall, because you can change trains easily from those hubs. Additionally, you should probably know that all the numbered subways were once IRT (Interborough Rapid Transit) lines, (with the lone exception of the "S" train, the 42nd Street Shuttle), and that the lettered trains were IND (Independent Subway System) and BMT (Brooklyn Manhattan Transit) lines, so if you get lost, and someone tells you, for example, "Take the IRT West Side Line", check your subway map, look for a numbered train on the west side, and you'll be okay. In this case, the train you'd be looking for would be the #1, #2, or #3 train. Or suppose someone was to tell you take the "BMT 14th Street Line". Check your map, and you'd find that it was the L train. Don't confuse the L train with the "EL" (elevated subway) in other parts of the city! One last major issue, pronounce Houston Street correctly! It is not pronounced the same way as the city in Texas, it is pronounced "How-ston". If you mispronounce Houston Street, people will certainly suspect that you are not a buff, but a poorly educated tourist! On another note, Houston Street is the equivalent of 0th Street, because 1st Street is immediately north, and named streets are immediately south, and also because there is an East Houston and West Houston Street. Also, in Brooklyn, there are numbered avenues too, so try not to get confused with Manhattan. In truth, Brooklyn's street grid is relatively similar to Manhattan's, at least on the west side of Brooklyn. The similarity is that there are named streets in Northern

Brooklyn and numbered streets in Southern Brooklyn, almost like a mirror image of Manhattan's street grid. So are you ready? Well, time to shake stuff down, borough by borough.

3

QUEENS

We begin in Queens of all places for a good reason. The reason is, Queens IS THE BOROUGH I HAVE THE LEAST KNOWLEDGE ABOUT!!!!! Noooooooooo! I have been to a few houses as firehouses are regularly called. So, here's a challenge I'm posing to you readers. Go find some firehouses in Queens, send me info about them afterwards, and then I'll publish it in the next edition.

So enough hoopla and *agita*, let's get started, right here now!

Engine Company 258, Ladder Company 115
10-40 47th Avenue.

Featured in the *AIA Guide to New York City*, Third Edition

This firehouse is a wonderful piece of architecture, that my dad and I visited in 1994. Engine 258 also carries a unique privilege; it is the only engine company outside of Manhattan that is a high-pressure company (high-pressure engines are engines specially designed to respond to high-rise fires and often placed in neighborhoods with a lot of high-rise buildings)! There are no other high-pressure engine companies in the outer boroughs! I suspect, although I have no information to back this up, that when high-rise fires break out in Midtown, Engine 258 is often special-called to help Manhattan's high-pressure engine companies deal with them (I've heard of Engine 212 in the Greenpoint section of Brooklyn near the Midtown Tunnel being special-called). The firehouse itself is not that far from the infamous "Pepsi-Cola" sign on the East River, and a short drive from the Queens-Midtown Tunnel.

Engine Company 287, Ladder Company 136, Battalion 46
86-53 Grand Avenue

Very little detail available other than a short visit in 1993. Battalion 46 though is one of the busiest battalions in Queens and in the city for that matter, and is also the home of many special companies, including Queens' rescue company, Rescue 4, Queens' satellite company, Satellite 4, and the city-wide Hazardous Materials Company, Haz-Mat 1, located at Squad 288's quarters. Not long ago Battalion 46 was the busiest battalion in the city! Buffs, send me more info please!

Engine Company 289, Ladder Company 138.
97-28 43rd Avenue.

Featured in the *AIA Guide to New York City*, Third Edition.

This firehouse is another piece of architecture, that we visited in 1992. It looks like Engine 258/Ladder 115 in some ways, but they were not designed by the same architect. Ladder 138 also carries the honor of being 1998's busiest ladder company in the city in terms of runs and workers, and runs a tower ladder. It is also in the famous Battalion 46 that I keep jabbering on about. This firehouse has a door into the firehouse built into one of the garage doors. It also looks like several other firehouses in Brooklyn and Queens, notably Engine 290/Ladder 103 on Sheffield Avenue in the East New York section of Brooklyn and Squad 270 /Division 13 in the Richmond Hill neighborhood in southern Queens.

Engine Company 292, Rescue Company 4
64-18 Queens Boulevard (FF Peter McLoughlin Way), between 64th/65th Streets

Author has particularly detailed knowledge, Author knows certain fire-fighters by name.

This firehouse, centrally located in the Woodside neighborhood of Queens, is a majestic presence towering above the traffic-choked Queens Boulevard and Brooklyn-Queens Expressway. Rescue Company 4 is one of the city's most elite companies. An assignment to Rescue 4 or any of the other Rescue companies is the equivalent of becoming an Army Ranger or a Navy SEAL, given that members of Rescue Companies must have at least 5 years on the job, have some special skill, and have had extensive training specifically so that they may be a member of a Rescue Company. To become a member of Rescue 4, a firefighter must request an interview with the captain of Rescue 4 and go through a probationary period on the company. Ultimately, the captain decides if the firefighter is worthy of being a member of the Rescue 4 (see also Manhattan-Rescue Company 1). Rescue 4 also uses special equipment, like the Hurst tool (FDNY colloquial for the Jaws of Life),life-saving rope (for rope rescues) and members of the rescue company are all certified as rescue divers for water rescue incidents. Furthermore, members of all the Rescue companies are responsible for going into fires and saving injured firefighters and civilians.

Engine 292 is nearly 90 years old, having been organized in 1913, originally as Engine 287's second piece. Five years later, the company was disbanded and reorganized as Engine 292 at 64-18 Queens Boulevard, where they have spent the past 80 years. Rescue 4 was organized, ironically enough, in 1931, some 18 years later. Rescue 4's response area is all working fires (in FDNY radio code, 10-75) in Queens and they may be special-called to certain parts of Northern Brooklyn like Greenpoint or Bushwick if necessary (Rescue 2, Brooklyn's Rescue Company is located in Central Brooklyn {Crown Heights}, and Brooklyn is a particularly large borough). They also are responsible for responding to any situation with unusual rescue operations, for example, an automobile accident, a water rescue, building collapse, or any other unusual rescue operations. Like the other rescue companies, they can be special-called to any place in the city if necessary. Engine 292 has two different names or mottoes, one is "Winfield Cougars", named for their part of Queens, Winfield, or the "Queens Boulevard La Casa de Loco" (The Crazy House). Rescue 4 doesn't have a particular motto, rather they have Popeye as their mascot and symbol. Except for a brief period from 1996-1997, Rescue 4 has always been at this firehouse on Queens Boulevard.

I visited this house on June 6, 2002, and met four firefighters by name, Firefighters Naviasky and Mahoney, and Lieutenant Roche (pronounced Rock) from Engine 292, and I also met the senior man on Rescue 4, Firefighter Mike Milner, who has 25 years on the job, and 18.5 with Rescue 4 alone! I also bought an Engine 292 shirt from these guys. The firehouse was also going through some renovation when I visited. Finally, I met one of the chiefs from Battalion 46 who was at the firehouse to examine the company log for Engine 292.

Both companies were prominently featured in the documentary "Brothers in Battle", made by the late Captain Brian Hickey of Rescue 4. Sadly, Captain Hickey was killed at the World Trade Center on September 11th. At my visit to the firehouse, Captain Hickey's funeral was set for the following Monday, and his widow, Donna Hickey, had called the firehouse also while I was visiting (of course I didn't listen in on the call, just heard that it was Donna Hickey).

On a happier note about "Brothers in Battle", the same Mike Milner that I met that day was one of the fires to receive a medal at Medal Day 1990 (one of the highlights in the documentary), specifically, the Emily Trevor Mary B. Warren Medal for his actions in rescuing a trapped woman in the infamous USAir 5050 plane crash on September 20th, 1989. He also was personally interviewed about what getting the medal meant to him, and he said, "The medal is a lifelong dream". Mike Milner evidently also has at least one other small claim to fame, he was mentioned in a story in Simon and Schuster's game *Firefighter*.

On another note, Rescue 4 was the only rescue company to have their rig survive September 11th completely intact. Admittedly, the rig had some bumps and bruises, but not to the extent that other Rescue companies had (Rescue 1 and 2 lost their rigs at the World Trade Center). On my visit however, they were running a spare rescue truck, but mainly because Rescue 4's normal rig was having scheduled maintenance. In fact, at this firehouse when I was visiting, Firefighter Naviasky, after hearing that I had written this book, called over the firehouse P.A. that I was in the housewatch. This firehouse is a great visit in Queens, and one of the best visits I've had! Go visit the "Winfield Cougars" and Popeye with his rescue truck!

Engine Company 320, Ladder Company 167

36-18 Francis Lewis Boulevard, near the Cross Island Parkway.

A beautiful, simple firehouse, the sister to many other firehouses like Engine 70/Ladder 53, and Ladder 3/Battalion 6, just to name a couple. This firehouse's patch is rather patriotic, with the American Flag on it. They call themselves "The Pride of Bayside", and their company patch is very patriotic. I used to visit this firehouse when I visited my Uncle Louie, who kept fig trees.

POSSIBLE TRIPS:

Engine 258/Ladder 115 would make a good combo with going to Midtown Manhattan Firehouses and/or firehouses in Northern Brooklyn (e.g. Greenpoint). Engine 292/Rescue 4 with Engine 287/Ladder 136/Battalion 46 and Engine 289/Ladder 138 are also good visits, given that they are within the same battalion. The #7 train (IRT Flushing Local) can take you to 61st Street-Woodside in Queens, and from there it is a modest walk to Engine 292/Rescue 4. Actually, Engine 292/Rescue 4 is not too hard to combine with Manhattan firehouses, mainly because the #7 train stops at major subway hubs like Grand Central Station (where one can catch the 4, 5, or 6 train or the 42nd Street Shuttle, the S train) and Times Square (where one can catch the A,C,E, N,Q,R,W, 1,2, or 3 trains, and where the #7 train has its western terminal).

Another good combo is Engine 320/Ladder 167 with some Bronx firehouses, and there's a huge Burgers/Ribs place near Engine 258/Ladder 115. Again, Queens is not really my specialty, so send in some info!

Engine 289/Ladder 138's quarters in the Corona section of Queens. It is very plain to see that the firehouse is very antique, especially with the green roof-work, reminiscent of Spanish architecture. It is also very difficult to see that this firehouse is actually Engine 289/Ladder 138's quarters, mainly because the lettering above the bay doors has faded, but if you look very closely, you can see it. (Henry Schneiderman Photo)

Engine 292/Rescue 4's quarters on Queens Boulevard in the Wood-side neighborhood of Queens. Except for a brief period in 1996-1997, both companies have always resided in this firehouse since their inceptions in 1913 and 1931 respectively. The seal of the City of New York is also visible between the two bays of the firehouse, and these two companies are probably the most famous in the Queens, also the subject of the late Captain Brian Hickey's documentary "Brothers in Battle", who was a member of Rescue 4. (Joseph Schnei-derman Photo)

A patriotic helmet worn by one of the members of Engine 292, taken in their quarters on Queens Boulevard. (Joseph Schneiderman Photo)

The logo and mascot of Rescue Company 4, Popeye, rendered in stained glass on the wall in their quarters. This piece of stained glass is on the same wall as all of the members of Rescue 4 who have recieved citations from the department for valor or other acts of courage or bravery. (Joseph Schneiderman Photo)

4

BROOKLYN

We've been to ten firehouses in Brooklyn, and they've all been dandies. Brooklyn has the most fire protection of any borough, namely 65 engine companies and 39 ladder companies, and is also home to 1999's busiest engine company and 1999's second busiest ladder company, which ironically enough, are quartered together, namely Engine 290 and Ladder 103 on Sheffield Avenue in East New York. If Brooklyn were a city on its own, it would be one of the largest ones in the nation. Brooklyn is a wonderful borough, it has everything, from parks, to malls, to museums, you name it! On some firehouses you can still see "BFD" inscribed in the woodwork or metal work, like Squad 252 in Bushwick, and Engine 204 in Cobble Hill. Heck, at one house on Rogers Avenue, namely Engine 249/Ladder 113, "Brooklyn Fire Dept." is still across the facade over the bays.

Well, let's get buffing!

Engine Company 205, Ladder Company 118
74-76 Middagh Street (Philip D'Adamo Place), at Henry Street

This firehouse is also of similar architecture to Engine 320/Ladder 167 and Ladder 3/Battalion 6, and sits a couple hundred yards from the base of the Brooklyn Bridge. This firehouse is also responsible not just for the Brooklyn Bridge and the neighborhoods of DUMBO (Down Under the Manhattan Bridge Overpass) and Fulton Landing, but also for the upscale neighborhood of Brooklyn Heights. Ladder 118 also is one of the last 12 ladder companies in the city to run a tiller ladder truck (a tractor trailer with one firefighter driving the back of the rig). The reason that they run one is most likely because in Brooklyn Heights, Fulton Landing, and DUMBO, there are a lot of small and tight streets (i.e. Cranberry Street, Willow Street, and Front Street, just to name a few), and tiller ladders are better suited for small, tight streets. Additionally, there are a fair amount of hills in that neighborhood (including the offramps and approaches to and from the Brooklyn and Manhattan Bridges), and tiller ladders are also well suited for hills. On another note, Ladder 118 was once the inhabitant of the famous "Jay Street Firehouse" in Downtown Brooklyn, when they were Ladder 68 in the time following the merger of the Brooklyn Fire Department with the FDNY, and finally in 1929, they moved in with Engine 205 to this house on Middagh Street. Engine 205 also is one of the few rigs, and for that matter vehicles in New York to still have the old yellow and black license plates, which I saw on my visit there on June 7, 2002, where I met a kind firefighter named Jesse. They read "ENG 205" ("eng" is a typical abbreviation for engine). It is a bit more common though to see FDNY rigs bearing license plates in Staten Island. The firehouse also an old street sign for Middagh Street on the inside of the firehouse at the housewatch. Engine 205 also has some historical valor in FDNY history. When horses were becoming phased out as the source of power to get FDNY rigs to and from the scenes of fires and whatever else the city sent them too, Engine 205 was given the honor or curse (you be the judge) of the last horse drawn run in FDNY history, which occurred on December 22nd, 1922, and was at Brooklyn Borough Hall, at Court and Joralemon Streets. It was a prearranged response so that they could pick up and begin to utilize a new motorized rig, but it was still the last horse-drawn response in FDNY history. The reason why they made the run as opposed to a company that protected that neighborhood also, like Engine 207 or Ladder 110 or Engine 226 (we'll get to those houses, hold your horses) is because back in the volunteer days of the Brooklyn Fire

Department, the company that is now Engine 205 was the first one to use a horse-drawn rig. The only equivalent event in the modern FDNY's history to Engine 205's last horsedrawn run is probably when Engine 164 in Staten Island replaced their Mack CF pumper with a Seagrave pumper which had been reassigned from Squad 18, which was the last front-line Mack CF in service, on March 17th, 2001. The reason for such an equivalency is the fact that from 1968 until 1989 the FDNY purchased Mack CF's for their engine companies on a very exclusive basis (only a few engines from that 21 year period did NOT run Mack CF's), and the FDNY had had a strong relationship with Mack dating back to the beginning of Mack in 1925, as Mack had built them engines, ladder trucks (tower ladders especially), rescue trucks, the Haz-Mat Unit, the Super Pumper (see also Brooklyn Engine 207/Ladder 110/Satellite 6/ FCU 1 and 2/Battalion 31/ Division 11), mask service units, wreckers, and other support units. On a different note, when Engine 205 was still making horsedrawn runs, they were quartered out of a firehouse on Pierrepoint (pronounced "Pier-point") Street, further south in Brooklyn Heights.

The block of Middagh Street (Philip D'Adamo Place) where the firehouse is located is named after the late Firefighter Philip D'Adamo of Ladder Company 118 who was killed in the line of duty on December 1st, 1984. We'll talk more about the renaming of streets at our next firehouse. This firehouse's motto is "Fire Under the Bridge", which makes perfect sense, given that they are almost under the Brooklyn Bridge! On my visit, I found that it was about a two or three minute walk to be under the Brooklyn Bridge. This firehouse is a wonderful visit to combine with Brooklyn Heights or Empire Fulton State Park or anything else in that area! Go visit these brothers fighting against "Fire Under the Bridge"!

Engine Company 207, Ladder Company 110, Satellite 6 (Maxi-Water Unit), Field Communications 1 and 2, 31st Battalion, 11th Division.

172 Tillary Street (Kevin Kane Place) at Gold Street at the off-ramp of the Brooklyn Queens-Expressway, near Flatbush Avenue Extension.

Author has particularly detailed knowledge, Authors knows certain fire-fighters by name.

Now this, my buffs, is a firehouse! It was built in 1971, and is one of the largest if not The largest firehouse in the city! It also has a police precinct neighbor, the 84th, and is right near the base of the Manhattan Bridge!

This firehouse is also literally right behind Fire Headquarters, at 9 MetroTech Center a short walk south on Gold Street and west on the Metrotech Plaza to Fire Headquarters.

This firehouse is a true buff's dream! Engine Company, Ladder Company, Specialty Units, a Battalion, and a Division, woo-hoo!

This firehouse is also the former home of the famous Super-Pumper, and part of that still lives on since the Maxi-Water Unit (Satellite 6) is a child of the Super Pumper System. Heck, all the Satellite companies are the children of the Super Pumper!

The Super Pumper actually carries a very nifty and unique story to it. The FDNY purchased it in 1965, and at the time, it was, and probably still is the most powerful land based fire engine on Earth! Some critics have called it "A Fireboat on Land", given that only fireboats could pump as much water as it could. It was designed by Mack, who had had a very storied relationship with the FDNY for nearly 60 or 70 years before the last Mack was purchased in 1989. It had to run two separate tractor-trailer fire engines because it was such a big piece, namely Super Pumper 1 which carried the water and pumps and monitors (more commonly known as deck guns), and Super Tender 1, which carried the hoses and more monitors and stuff. The Satellites actually originally were rigs that carried more equipment for the Super Pumper and Super Tender and operated on major fires also and carried water. The truth is though, that although the Super Pumper system may have been designed for major fires like 10-60's (FDNY radio code for a major disaster), it was truly designed if the Russians poisoned New York's water supply during the Cold War. The Super Pumper carried about 10,000 gallons of water, and probably with the proper filtering, all that water could be converted to drinking water. The Super Pumper did operate at major fires though, and ultimately in 1982, the company was disbanded and the rigs were disposed of. The Super Pumper though is a big subject in many books about fire engines, more notably a book called *Services Not Required*, which tells the stories of special companies that served in the FDNY that were ultimately disbanded as the years passed. The FDNY currently runs six Satellite Companies, one in each borough except for Brooklyn, which runs Satellite 6 out of this firehouse and Satellite 3 out of Engine 284/ Ladder 149's house, which is further south. All of the Satellite Companies are based on the Super-Pumper, in the sense that they carry over-sized monitors, carry a lot of hoses, and can pump a lot of water quickly. The engine companies that run with the Satellite companies actually run 2000 gallon per minute pumpers, which is the case with Engine 207's rig. Speaking of their rig, an image of an old rig of theirs (1979) was featured in the Simon and Schuster game *Firefighter*.

To tell the truth, I actually don't understand why Engine 207 doesn't run a 2000 gallon per minute high pressure pumper (a nifty combination and probably never even theorized by the FDNY), given that there are a fair amount of high-rises currently and going up in Downtown Brooklyn, and Engine 207 could easily be special-called to Lower Manhattan for a major high-rise conflagration. That would probably be as dynamic, unique, and as ground-breaking a rig as the Super Pumper, given that it would serve a double purpose: high-rise fire protection and a companion to a Satellite. FDNY, give it some thought!

On my last visit to this firehouse, namely June 5 and 6, 2002, some very special things happened. First of all, I met three firefighters by name, Dave, Jeff and Matt (I didn't catch their last names, C'est la vie), and they gave me the official department master list of divisions and battalions and company locations! I also purchased a long-sleeved September 11th memorial shirt, commemorating the five men from that house who died that fateful day and Battalion Chief Dennis Cross of Battalion 57 (which is in Division 11, see also Brooklyn Engine 219/Ladder 105) and Captain Timothy Stackpole of Ladder 103, evidently a more famous member of Brooklyn's firefighters and a member of Division 11 (even though Ladder 103 is in Division 15). Also, the firehouse's area on Tillary Street is called "Kevin Kane Place", named in memorial after the late Kevin Kane of Ladder 110 who died on September 13th, 1991. Evidently, Kevin Kane's influence was far reaching in the department, as Marine Company 6's boat is named the Kevin C. Kane, in honor of him. This practice is actually common in the department, or at least, I know that the block of E. 176th Street in the Bronx where Rescue 3 is quartered is renamed after a member of that company who was killed in the line of duty, an Alfred E. Ronaldson, and the block was subsequently renamed Alfred E. Ronaldson Place, and also had a fireboat named after him (which now is no longer in service), and we've seen Philip D'Adamo Place at Engine 205/Ladder 118. Additionally, I found out that Ladder 110 had another slogan aside from "Tillary Street Tigers", namely "Fort Greene Cavalry". The firehouse as a whole is also known as "The Island of Misfit Toys", which comes from the fact that they run an engine, ladder, satellite, field com units, battalion and divsion, which is a very wide diversity of rigs and companies. Also, I found that Engine 207 is one of the oldest companies in the city, having served Brooklyn since 1869, and ironically enough, that Ladder 110 celebrated its 110th anniversary in 2001! Speaking of history, Ladder 110 was also the first ladder company in the city to run a metal aerial ladder in the early 1950's. The best part though was on my visit on the afternoon of June 5th, the engine caught an EMS (Emergency Medical Services) run, and Dave offered to let me ride with them on their run! He told me that they had an extra seat and that I could ride with them. I politely said no, because at the time, in ten years of buffing, I'd never been offered to go on a run with the guys, and I wasn't sure if my beloved parents would approve. My parents actually were proud that I had the sense to say no, but said that if the firefighters offered to let me go with them on an EMS run again, I could. Additionally, I saw the gantry that would have hung above their old firehouse on

Jay Street, which is in the back of their current firehouse. This firehouse will forever have a very special place in my heart!

On a separate note, Engine 207 and Ladder 110's response area is all of Downtown Brooklyn, which includes Metrotech Center, New York State Supreme Court, Brooklyn Borough Hall, the Fulton Mall, and some housing. Additionally, the "Tillary Street Tigers", as they are known, are responsible for certain parts of DUMBO and Fort Greene, and some of Brooklyn Heights. Satellite 6 is also dispatched on all Second Alarms that Engine 207 rolls on. The 31st Battalion is responsible for Downtown Brooklyn, the famous Brooklyn Navy Yard, some parts of southern Williamsburg, and is actually a hub of city-wide fire operations. For example, the city-wide arson headquarters is located at Engine 211/Ladder 119's quarters on Hooper Street, which is in the 31st Battalion, the city-wide photo unit is based out of the same firehouse, and two of the three Field Communications Units are based out of Engine 207/Ladder 110's house. Division 11 is responsible for all of Northern Brooklyn, including Brooklyn Heights, Bedford-Stuyvesant, the Brooklyn Navy Yard, Downtown Brooklyn, Greenpoint, Williamsburg, and Prospect Park, just to name a few neighborhoods. Division 11 also is home to Brooklyn's Communications office, Squad 1, The Research and Development Division, and the "Hi-Ex Foam Unit" (a large capacity foam pumper), located at Engine 212's quarters in Greenpoint.

This firehouse, although it is in a relatively central, and busy location, is a wonderful place to stop off. It is also close enough to the Brooklyn Bridge that one could walk the Brooklyn Bridge from that firehouse. Although the firehouse is truly at the base of the Manhattan Bridge, both bridges are easily accessible! Go visit this granddaddy of firehouses, the "Tillary Street Tigers", and be sure to ask about the Super Pumper! Maybe with luck you'll meet Dave, Jeff, or Matt!

Engine Company 210
160 Carlton Avenue

Visited in 1997 with visit to Brooklyn Museum. Author requests readers to send in more information.

One of the many solo engine companies in New York City, also one of those many firehouses tucked in between buildings. This firehouse is one of several firehouses I have seen with the front door to the firehouse incorporated into the garage door! Nifty! This firehouse was also Rescue 2's home for many many years, aside from the Jay Street Firehouse and their current house on Bergen Street. On my visit to Engine 207/Ladder 110/Satellite 6/FCU 1 and 2/Battalion 31/Division 11, my friends there told me that this firehouse was under renovation, and that Engine 210 had been temporarily relocated to Engine 211/Ladder 119's quarters on Hooper Street in southern Williamsburg near the Navy Yard. Just a warning, for all of you who stop and find construction going on. Please, buffs, give me more info!

Engine Company 219, Ladder Company 105
494 Dean Street

Same visit date as Engine 210. Author requests readers to send in more information.

It is a relatively modern firehouse, protecting some of the more beautiful and interesting parts of Brooklyn, and is a wonderful visit. Ladder 105 also is presently operating a unique rig: a Spartan Aerialscope Demonstrator, different from the standard Seagrave Aerialscopes or Mack CF Baker-Aerialscopes used by the other tower ladders. There actually is a certain amount of irony to the fact that Ladder 105 runs a Spartan Demonstrator, given that like Ladder 1 and Ladder 119, in the early days of the tower ladder, they ran a similar rig (a Mack C with boom work by Truco, see also Manhattan Engine 7/Ladder 1/Battalion 1). This firehouse is also part of the 57th Battalion, which is mainly responsible for Bedford Stuyvesant and Bushwick.

Engine Company 224

274 Hicks Street, between Joralemon and State Streets.

Featured in the *AIA Guide to New York City,* Third Edition.

This is another fine piece of architecture, a big beauty, like many of the other solo companies, sandwiched in between buildings. At one time, like the other firehouses in the city, they had doors that opened inwards, not upward like conventional garage doors. The firehouse is also situated in the prestigious and beautiful neighborhood of Brooklyn Heights. The other architecture in Brooklyn Heights is worth a look, and there are many little shops and things that are fun. Engine 224 actually was one of those companies that did NOT run a Mack CF as we discussed with Engine 205/Ladder 118. For a while, or at least on our first visit there back in 1992 or 1993 (I can't remember exactly, I have a photo), they ran an American LaFrance pumper. On my last, visit the firehouse was having some renovation done. Go visit these protectors of Brooklyn Heights!

Engine Company 226

409 State Street, between Bond/Nevins Streets

Featured in the *AIA Guide to New York City,* Third Edition, Author requests readers to send in more information.

This firehouse, like many others in the city, including many in Brooklyn, is sandwiched between buildings. Engine 226 is responsible Downtown Brooklyn, and the neighborhoods of Boerum Hill, Carroll Gardens, and Cobble Hill, just to name a couple. This firehouse sits in a rather picturesque neighborhood, and is also part of the 31st Battalion. Engine 226 also dates back to before the turn of the century, specifically, 1889. Engine 226 also was where Edwin (Ed) Schneider, the subject of his book *A Fire Chief Remembers* (see For Further Reference "A") served as Captain upon his promotion to that rank in 1944. He evidently still has or had strong ties to Engine 226, as a present portrait of their company at the time of his book's publication (1992) was seen in his book. This firehouse was also one of many from Brooklyn to be affected by the events of September 11th, and a photo of their firehouse taken in the wake of the attacks actually won a Pulitzer Prize. On my visit on June 5, 2002, the firehouse door had an American flag painted on it, and many memorials had been placed by people from the neighborhood. On a better note, the firehouse is painted a wonderful shade of rustic red, which blends in well with the neighborhood. Not far from the Fulton Mall and other sites in Downtown Brooklyn, this firehouse is a wonderful visit.

Engine Company 240, 48th Battalion
1309 Prospect Avenue.

Featured in the *AIA Guide to New York City*, Third Edition. Author requests readers to send in more information.

This firehouse could easily be mistaken for a little residential house were it not for its garage door. It is very similar to Engine 320/Ladder 167 in Queens, but there are subtle differences, which one will notice upon arriving. It is also the only building mentioned specifically in the Windsor Terrace neighborhood in the AIA Guide! When arriving at the firehouse, one will immediately notice a tower above the firehouse. That was from the days when fires were spotted by the fire department through watchtowers and then the department responded. Engine 240 was also one of the last companies to replace their Mack CF pumper truck with the now standard-issue Seagrave. It fits very well into the neighborhood. Engine 240 also carries the honor of being one of several companies in the outer that is 100 years old or older (1896-1996). The 48th Battalion is also the current home of the famous Squad Company 1, who is quartered on Union Street near Grand Army Plaza at the northwest edge of Prospect Park in the now disbanded Engine 269's FQ. The battalion's responsibility is neighborhoods like Prospect Park and Windsor Terrace and some of the more beautiful areas of Brooklyn aside from Brooklyn Heights. The 48th Battalion is also where Ed Schneider of the book *A Fire Chief Remembers* (see For Further Reference "A") buffed as a teenager (in his case, visiting the firehouse and riding with them), and later served as acting battalion chief and while he was a captain, and later full battalion chief after his promotion, in ironically enough, 1948, before his ultimate assignment to Battalion 42 in the Bay Ridge/Coney Island neighborhood. This firehouse, when the Brooklyn Fire Department was still in service before Brooklyn merged with the City of New York, was the home of Engine 40 of the Brooklyn Fire Department, which became Engine 240, and Ladder 21, whose fate I am not aware of (Ladder 121 is currently in Queens). The firehouse also has a sort of fraternal twin, the aforementioned Engine 249/Ladder 113 in another part of Brooklyn. And for the kids, after they've visited, there's a playground right across Ocean Parkway/Prospect Expressway.

Engine Company 241, Ladder Company 109
6630 3rd Avenue

This a modern firehouse, and the B39 bus runs near there, as does the R subway line (along 4th Avenue.). They call themselves the "3rd Avenue Express", which is fitting given their location. Ironically enough, Engine 239, quartered on 4th Avenue near Prospect Park, call themselves the "4th Avenue Express"! Engine 241 also is one of the few companies in the outer boroughs who are 100 years old or more (1896-1996, like Engine 240). Originally, before their current firehouse was built in 1971, they were quartered on Bay Ridge Avenue. A wonderful trip in Bay Ridge!

Engine Company 242
9219 5th Avenue, between 92nd/94th Streets

Author requests readers to send in more information.

This firehouse, "The Pride of Bay Ridge", is one of the southernmost if not the southernmost firehouse in Brooklyn. The Verrazano Narrows Bridge towers over their part of Bay Ridge. This firehouse is also located in Division 8, which covers Staten Island and three battalions in Brooklyn. This firehouse is also the home of R.A.C. (Rehabilitation and Comfort) 5. On major fires, i.e. a Third Alarm, R.A.C. units will be dispatched to provide the firefighters with water, food, and other small things to combat fatigue that the firefighters are experiencing. R.A.C.'s 1 and 2 are always in service, but R.A.C.'s 3-5 are only in service between May and September. This firehouse also is the only one where I have seen to have the company motto on the facade above the garage doors. In fact, I'm amazed that nobody has written a book on that firehouse called "Firefighters from The Pride of Bay Ridge and the Great Blue Bridge", given how close the firehouse is to the Verrazano Narrows Bridge and how public interest in the FDNY has shot up since September 11th! Go visit "The Pride of Bay Ridge", and maybe you'll write just such a book!

Engine Company 276, Ladder Company 156, Battalion 33
1635 East 14th Street

This firehouse protected my dad when he grew up in Brooklyn! He grew up right down 14th Street from it! At present, they protect some beautiful old brownstones and some of the tenements that have replaced those old brownstones, including, where my dad grew up. The 33rd Battalion also carries the honor of being in Division 15, which protects some of the more harder hit parts of the city, like East New York, New Lots Avenue, and Crown Heights. Go visit these protectors of a quieter part of the very very busy 15th Division!

Briefly, let's establish one out-of-service firehouse that's worth a visit! This famous house is the "**Jay Street Firehouse**", a.k.a. the former Brooklyn Fire Headquarters, a.k.a. the former quarters (F.Q.) of Ladder 118, also the F.Q. of Rescue 2, located at 365 Jay Street. This firehouse is a towering presence on Jay Street, and it is a wonderful visit if visiting Brooklyn Heights or the Downtown Brooklyn Area. Although no longer used as a firehouse, it is a memoir to the firehouse of years past, and it has a very cathedral-like tower. It also was the FQ of Engine 207, Ladder 110 and Battalion 31 at one time, from 1947 until their new firehouse on

Tillary Street was built in 1971. This firehouse also was the home of Searchlight 2. In the days before high powered lights became readily available on fire engines, the FDNY ran Searchlight units. In the case of Searchlight 2, they had a unique piece of apparatus, namely a modified Packard sedan with searchlights on it, which was built in 1930. One can actually read more about it and see a photo of it in the book *Fire Engines in North* America (see also For Further Reference "A").This firehouse also bears a plaque on it, because it is one of the buildings that the City of New York preserves through its historical society. The firehouse is also directly across the street from the New York City Transit Authority headquarters on Jay Street. Situated directly above the Jay Street-Borough Hall subway station, it represents history, the fire department, the City of New York and the City of Brooklyn all rolled into one!

Now, now that we've established some firehouses, here are some

POSSIBLE TRIPS!

Engine 207/Ladder 110, Engine 224, Engine 226, Fire Headquarters, The Jay Street Firehouse, The Brooklyn Heights Promenade, and the Downtown Brooklyn shopping. I would recommend also that if you visit Engine 207/Ladder 110 or 224 or both to take the B61 bus line up to Williamsburg to Peter Luger's Steak House at 178 Broadway! This 100-year-old steak house is well worth it! It would make a wonderful post-buffing or pre-buffing trip! Although you can only pay cash, because following they do not take credit cards, it is worth it! The steaks are wonderful, the environment is nostalgic and fitting for a Steak House, and not just the steak is good! The fried potatoes rule!

Another trip in that area is a visit to the Transit Museum. And although this specific trip probably can't happen until 2003, because the Transit Museum is presently closed for renovation, is the Downtown Brooklyn shopping, Engine 207/Ladder 110, the Transit Museum, and the Jay Street Firehouse. The Transit Museum is located in the old IND Court Street subway station, and still has turnstiles to get in. If you want to purchase transit related memorabilia, Grand Central Station currently is the home of the store that normally is at the museum. Among the more interesting items is a neck-tie with the subway numbers and letters on it against a black background. And the best part about this trip in Downtown Brooklyn: You can walk it all!

In Brooklyn Heights alone, the Promenade, Engine 205/Ladder 118 and Engine 224 are all good visits. Near Engine 205/Ladder 118 is the River Cafe, at 1 Water Street, an upscale little restaurant. One of the best reasons to go there despite its expensiveness is a nifty little chocolate confection called "The Brooklyn Bridge". It is actually what it sounds like: a Chocolate Mousse, edible, model of the Brooklyn Bridge. Also in that area is a nice ice cream parlor located at Marine Company 7's former quarters at the foot of Old Fulton Street. However, I would advise against walking in the neighborhood known as DUMBO. It is a particularly ratty neighborhood, and I personally fail to see its appeal to artists. However, there are some nice places to walk closer to the Brooklyn Bridge and in Brooklyn Heights. Heck, if you're a big walking type of person, you can walk between the following firehouses in a relatively short amount of time (you make your own walking tours!!):Engine 205/ Ladder 118, Engine 207/Ladder 110, Engine 224, Engine 226, and "The Jay Street Firehouse". Just make sure that you have plenty of water (there's a newsstand in the Jay Street—Borough Hall subway station which sells bottled water), and there are plenty of little stores around where you can buy bottled water. Speaking of subway stations, built into the Clark Street-Brooklyn Heights subway station is a little market (or maybe the subway station is built into it, you decide). Although I didn't actually go into the market, I'd recommend that hungry or thirsty buffs pay them a visit.

Another trip outside of that area is going to Engine 241/Ladder 109 and combining it with a visit to a little restaurant-bar called Salty Dog at 75th and 3rd Avenue of Brooklyn. Salty Dog has an old Mack fire engine in it, and is a fire buff's place! It is worth a visit. If you've been to Peter Luger's, wait at least eight hours between meals! Also, people who are sensitive to smokers should not go, as there are smokers there. The best route there is the R train to 77th street station and a short walk north on 4th Avenue and then across 75th to 3rd. Furthermore, one can visit Engine 242 off that same subway line, by taking the R to its terminal at

95th Street. Although the subway station itself is a little bit cruddy, it is a two block walk north on 5th Avenue to Engine 242. Also, down on the corner of 5th Avenue and 94th Street, there is a small pizzeria, Espresso Pizzeria, which probably has one of the best meal deals in the city, a big slice of pizza with any topping and a small soda for $1.50! It costs that much to ride the subway or buses one way!

Additionally, combining Engine 210 or Engine 219/Ladder 105 with the Brooklyn Museum would be a nice trip. Check out the subways and buses. Unfortunately, although I try to know the system well, I don't quite know it like the palm of my hand. Another good trip combo is a visit to Fort Greene or Prospect Park and Engine 240/Battalion 48 or Engine 276/Ladder 156/Battalion 33. There is also plenty of beautiful architecture in both firehouses' jurisdiction, so check that out too!

Remember, send me info on your buffing! So, have fun in Brooklyn, the big borough!!

Engine 205/Ladder 118's quarters on Middagh Street (Philip D'Adamo Place) in Brooklyn Heights. The black flags denoting the death of firefighters obfuscate the fact that this is Engine 205/Ladder 118's quarters. This firehouse, like so many others in the city, lost firefighters on September 11th, and in addition to the black flags, the American flag is still being flown at half-mast. This firehouse was constructed after Engine 205 carried out the last horse-drawn run in FDNY history. If you look closely, you can see their logo on the right side of the firehouse. (Joseph Schneiderman Photo)

Engine 205's rig backing into quarters on June 7th, 2002. All engine companies carry a small ladder (no more than 40 feet or so) in the event that the fire is small enough that they don't need a ladder company to respond with them but still need to be off the ground in fire-fighting operations. The deck gun, or monitor is also visible in this photo (right center roughly), which is used on heavy volumes of fire. The hosebed is also seen here, with varying lengths of hose for varying volumes of fire, like the 1.75 inch, the 2.5, and 3.5. Fire engines also carry first aid equipment and defibrilators (for heart attack victims), and the famous Scott-Paks (breathing apparatus). Finally, if you look very closely, you can see Engine 205 and Ladder 118's logo, and even closer, you can see the outline of a tower of the Brooklyn Bridge on that logo. (Joseph Schneiderman Photo)

The Deputy Chief's car for Division 11, taken at Division 11's quarters on Tillary Street in Downtown Brooklyn. In the FDNY, a Deputy Chief is the same as a Division Chief, and Division Commanders (still with the rank of Deputy Chief) wear stars on their collars, like generals in the armed services. The car is a Ford Crown Victoria, but without a lightbar. Sometimes Deputy Chiefs will ride in Chevrolet Surbubans or Ford Excursion like Battalion Chiefs, but normally, they will be in this car or the Division Van, which is just what it sounds like, a diesel powered van. The Field Communications Unit can be seen in the background. (Joseph Schneiderman Photo)

The Maxi-Water Unit, also known as Satellite 6, taken in quarters, also on Tillary Street in Downtown Brooklyn. Ironically enough, although the Satellite system ultimately replaced the Super Pumper System, Satellite 6 now is housed in the same apparatus bay that the Super Pumper and Super Tender were quartered in. (Joseph Schneiderman Photo)

Engine 210's quarters on Carlton Avenue in the Fort Greene section of Brooklyn. Note the door inside the firehouse garage door. Currently, this firehouse is being renovated, but one of its' claim to fame is being Rescue 2's quarters for many many years, and the portrait of their rig would be outside of this firehouse. (Henry Schneiderman Photo)

Engine 219/Ladder 105's quarters on Dean Street. At the time this photo was taken, Ladder 105 was on a run. Note the lack of windows on the facade above the garage door. (Henry Schneiderman Photo)

Engine 224's quarters on Hicks Street in Brooklyn Heights. Note the green roof, in the style of Spanish architecture, like Engine 210's quarters in Fort Greene. Note also the brick work done on the sides of their quarters. This firehouse was also featured in the *AIA Guide to New York City*. (Joseph Schneiderman Photo)

Engine 226's quarters on State Street near the Fulton Mall. This firehouse also lost men on September 11th, and like several other of the solo companies (engine or otherwise), they are flying an American Flag across the facade of the firehouse. On a better note, note the rustic red color of their firehouse, also featured in the *AIA Guide to New York City.* (Joseph Schneiderman Photo)

Engine 242's quarters on 5th Avenue in Bay Ridge. Unlike many of its kind, this firehouse is fairly wide for being sandwiched between buildings. Also unlike many of its kind, this firehouse is only two stories tall,as many of the firehouses sandwiched between buildings, especially the older ones are three, sometimes four stories tall. If you look very closely, you can see "The Pride of Bay Ridge" in the sign denoting that this is a firehouse. (Joseph Schneiderman Photo)

Fire Headquarters at 9 Metrotech Center in Downtown Brooklyn. Although this is not a firehouse, it is still worth noting, if nothing else, because the senior staff of the department, like the Fire Commissioner, the First Deputy Commissioner, the Chief of Department, and the Chief of Operations all call this low-rise against high-rises their base of operations. (Joseph Schneiderman Photo)

5

THE BRONX!

Ah, the Bronx. Home of the New York Yankees, and much of my family! The Bronx is also the setting of the famous book *Report from Engine Company 82* by Dennis Smith. Although I have never been to Engine 82, I know where it is, 1213 Intervale Avenue at 169th, and I have been to 14 other firehouses, and this is the profile on them!

Well, enough fuzzy stuff. Time for some hardcore buffing!

Engine Company 38, Ladder Company 51
3446 Eastchester Road

Author has particularly detailed knowledge. Author knows particular firefighter(s) here by name.

This firehouse is another twin to Engine 320/Ladder 167, and they run a tower ladder, and have the lowest number for any engine company in the Bronx. On Sundays, they trained near Michelangelo Junior High School just off Gun Hill Road by I-95. I once went up in the bucket of the tower ladder, back when it was a Mack/Aerialscope. Engine 38 originally was based in Manhattan back in the early days of the department, but they were disbanded and later reorganized and sent to the Bronx. Currently, this firehouse is responsible for a fair amount of the Northern Bronx.

This firehouse also is the only one I know of to put my picture on the walls! After I went up in the tower ladder, we sent them a blown-up photo of me on the tower ladder, and they hung it on the wall! Thus, it is very dear to me and my family.

Engine Company 45, Ladder Company 58, 18th Battalion
924–926 East Tremont Avenue

Author requests readers to send in more information.

I don't remember much about this firehouse aside from seeing it on a return trip from Yankee Stadium, but it's worth a visit. Engine 45 is technically the company on the site, but a new firehouse was built next door, with an adjoining wall for Ladder 58 and the 18th Battalion. Engine 45 was also a victim or participant (you be the judge, see also Squad Company 41) in the FDNY's experiment with chartreuse. Ladder 58 also was the only fire engine of any kind from New York City to be featured in the book "Fire Trucks in Action". The famous Squad Company 1 was run out of these quarters during the tumultuous "Burning Bronx" of the '70s, from 1972 to their disbandment in 1976. Squad 1 was reorganized in 1977 in Brooklyn, however.

Engine Company 46, Ladder Company 27
460 Cross Bronx Expressway (access road, not on the highway itself)

Aside from seeing their mural from the Cross Bronx Expressway, I don't know much about these guys either. I do know they are called the "Cross Bronx Express", but go visit and send me info!

Engine Company 48, Ladder Company 56, Division 7
2417 Webster Avenue

Though I have visited I know very little about this house. I do however know that they have been on Webster Avenue for a while, initially farther north, and that one of their firefighters from Engine 48 was recently featured on a documentary on PBS chronicling firefighters in the Bronx, called appropriately enough, "Firemen in the Bronx". Division 7 is responsible for protecting the northern half of the Bronx, including neighborhoods like Riverdale, Belmont, Wakefield, and Pelham Bay Park, which is compromised of six battalions. Division 7 also protects Fordham University, and is also responsible for a battalion in Manhattan, namely Battalion 13, which protects Inwood and the George Washington Bridge and all of Manhattan north of 160th Street. But again, I know very little about the house! Please send me info!

Engine Company 63, Battalion 15
755 East 233rd Street

Author has particularly detailed knowledge.

One of the northernmost firehouses in the city, the 15th Battalion calls itself the "Top of Da' Bronx", and with good reason. It is a typical municipal building, with something of a tower on it. Although I don't believe there is a correlation, the tower could mean they are not only the "Top of Da' Bronx" but at least locally, the top of the city! Battalion 15 has a unique statistic about its' ladder companies, they run one of each different ladder truck currently used the FDNY. Specifically, a tiller ladder (Ladder 39), a tower ladder (Ladder 51), and an aerial ladder (Ladder 61). Recently, Engine 63 and Battalion 15's motto became "Wakefield Warriors" and "Top of Da' Bronx"! Go visit!

Engine Company 66, Ladder Company 61
21 Asch Loop West in Co-op City

Author has particularly detailed knowledge.

Co-op City's fire protection, it is a modern firehouse with Ladder 61 being an aerial ladder. This firehouse is also a part of the aforementioned 15th Battalion. Their slogan is "The Bronx Vikings". It protects not only these huge apartments, but also some of the more suburban parts of the city, and more northern parts, and stands out in a neighborhood of malls and high-rise apartment buildings. And believe it or not, the back end of the firehouse is visible from the New England Thruway. You have to look closely, but at an on-ramp on the northbound side, you can just spot it as the little building amongst big buildings. Check it out!

Engine Company 69 (FQ), Ladder Company 39
243 East 233rd Street.

Featured in the *AIA Guide to New York City*, Third Edition.

Engine 69 is now in Manhattan. Ladder 39 is now one of the northernmost companies in the city, almost in Westchester County. Ladder 39 happens to be the only solo ladder company in the Bronx, and one of the 12 remaining tiller-ladders left in New York City. Engine 69 was unfortunately featured in the Necrology section (Demolished Buildings) of the AIA guide, but they have a future in Manhattan, quartered with Ladder 28 and the 16th Battalion. Ladder 39 now protects that part of the Bronx, in Woodlawn. They were called at one time "Thriller Tiller", and are currently called "The Pride of Woodlawn". At one time they were quartered with Engine 63/Battalion 15 on the other side of 233rd Street, and are still a part of Battalion 15.

Engine Company 70, Ladder Company 53
169 Schofield Street, on City Island

Author has particularly detailed knowledge.

City Island's fire protection, an engine and a tower ladder. At one time Engine 70 was a "Squrt", that is, it had a 40-foot or so boom to shoot water with a ladder. Later Engine 70 became a "Tele-Squrt". It is another sibling to Engine 320/Ladder 167 in Queens, and every now and then, you might see a vehicle from the Pelham Fire Dept. or one of the other towns in Westchester. During the budget crunch of the 70's, these companies were disbanded and reorganized a couple of times, and the first time they were disbanded, a figment of the FDNY's past replaced them on City Island, namely "Combination Fire Company 121". In the old days of the FDNY, engine companies were known as the "Combination Engine Company", because they carried water, hoses, and ran a ladder truck. Well, this idea (which evidently did not work for some reason, the combination engine company concept returned to plain old engine companies not long after they developed it) came back to protect City Island for a while, and it also came back in Staten Island (in truth, it came back all over, those boroughs mainly) at Engine 151/Ladder 76, who were disbanded and temporarily became "Combination Fire Company 131". Engine 70 and Ladder 53 also carry the unusual honor of being the quietest fire companies in the city, meaning that they get the least number of runs. They call themselves "Fantasy Island", and despite the fact that they don't get runs, they are probably one of the more famous companies. Even so, they still get their share of runs. Go visit!

Engine Company 71, Ladder Company 55, Division 6
720 Melrose Avenue, at East 155th Street.

Author requests readers to send in more information.

A modern looking firehouse, in the southern nook of the Bronx, not far from Yankee Stadium and Bronx Borough Hall. Engine 71 is an old company, meaning that they go back to the 19th century. Engine 71 also had been quartered on Park Avenue in the Bronx (yes, there is a Park Avenue in the Bronx, not quite as fashionable as Manhattan's), and called themselves "Pride of Park Avenue". They also have called themselves and still call themselves "War Wagon". Their firehouse is located in the 14th Battalion, which protects all of the Bronx south of 161st Street, including Mott Haven, "The Hub", and Port Morris. Certain companies from Battalion 14 (like this house) may also be special-called to Yankee Stadium, even though Yankee Stadium's official fire protection (Engine Company 68/Ladder Company 49) is located in another battalion (the 17th) and further northwest, specifically, on Ogden Avenue. Division 6 is responsible for the southern half of the Bronx, which includes some of the busiest parts of the city, like Morrisania, Mott Haven, Highbridge, and Hunts Point just to name a couple of neighborhoods. They are also responsible for a battalion in Manhattan just like Division 7, namely Battalion 16, which protects the eastern part of Harlem and Manhattan above 125th Street. Ladder 55 also had Garfield or some other large cartoon cat as their logo for some time, and like many other firehouses in the South Bronx, their patch said "SOUTH BRONX" on it. And they were at one time quartered across town at our next station...

Engine Company 72, Satellite Company 2
3929 East Tremont Avenue

Featured in the *AIA Guide to New York City*, Third Edition. Author has particularly detailed knowledge thanks to kind tours by firefighters. Author knows particular firefighter(s) here by name.

One of the few firehouses with a triple crown of our categories, it is a modern looking firehouse which protects Pelham Bay Park and the two major bridges, the Throgs Neck and the Whitestone, and is centrally located between both. The Satellite is also the only Satellite company in the Bronx.

Engine 72 has an unusual history, as they were once a Manhattan company near Union Square, then they were disbanded, then they found a home in the Bronx. Their rig and members after their disbandment became Engine (now Squad) 41's second rig when the Bronx suffered through heavy arson and fires in the 70's. Speaking of rigs, Engine 72 was also one of the last companies in the city to replace their Mack CF pumper. The FDNY legacy of Macks continues on, though, in Satellite 2's rig, as with the other satellite companies. Ladder 55 was quartered at this firehouse at one time, and on the facade above the garage doors it says, "ENGINE 72 LADDER". This firehouse also has the pole column (yes, they do have a pole) visible from the outside. Like the other engine companies running satellite companies, Engine 72 runs a 2000 gallon per minute pumper. It is one of the closer ones to my grandmother, and it's a wonderful visit. Go see it! Although their symbol was once a bird wearing a helmet ready to fight fire, they have since changed their symbol, now to the view looking up to the Throgs Neck Bridge with an eagle on top against a sunset background. But their slogan hasn't changed, which they really do live up to,namely, "Never a Dull Moment".

Engine Company 89, Ladder Company 50
2924 Bruckner Boulevard (northbound), at Crosby Avenue

Author has particularly detailed knowledge thanks to kind tours by firefighters. Author knows particular firefighter(s) here by name.

Another one near Pelham Bay Park, is the "Cuckoo's Nest" as they call themselves on their patch. One reason they probably call themselves the "Cuckoo's Nest" is their proximity to Long Island Sound. They are another twin to Engine 320/Ladder 167. They are also a wonderful visit, as they are sandwiched between Catholic Schools and stores, and they run a tower ladder too. Both companies also have always been on this firehouse on Bruckner Boulevard since 1926. Ladder 50's tower ladder is also somewhat unique, at least on my last visit, they were running a four-door Mack CF/Aerialscope with current FDNY colors. The uniqueness there is that many of those older tower ladders are just red and white as opposed to red, white, yellow and gold. Ladder 50 also is one of three 95 foot tower ladders in Division 7, the others being Ladder 58 (which we visited also!) and Ladder 33, as opposed to just one in Division 6 (Ladder 44). Go visit the "Cuckoo's Nest"!

Engine Company 97
1454 Astor Avenue

Author requests readers to send in more information.

These guys are the "Astor Avenue Hilton", but I don't know much about them, aside from their location near Albert Einstein Hospital. Engine 97 also happens to be the largest two digit engine company in the department (Engines 98-150 were never organized, the next highest number is 151 in Staten Island). They also are the quarters to BFU (Brush Fire Unit) 8, one of only three BFU's not in Staten Island.

Squad Company 41
330 East 150th Street

Featured in the *AIA Guide to New York City*, Third Edition. Author requests readers to send in more information.

A little piece of architecture, sandwiched between other buildings. A Squad for Harlem and the Western Bronx, they are a busy company! Their responsibility in Harlem is Battalions 11, 12, 13, and 16, which are all the battalions there are in Harlem and extreme upper Manhattan (even parts of the Upper West Side!!!), and Battalions 13 and 16 are in Bronx Divisions, as aforementioned. The firehouse itself is actually quartered in the 14th Battalion, though. In 1989, they were disbanded, and fires in their neighborhood shot up, and after the citizens of the neighborhood came knocking on City Hall's door asking for the return of their fire protection, the then Engine 41 was reorganized and assigned a special rig, making them "Advanced Engine Company 41". I've seen somebody on the Internet actually develop a Lego fire engine based on Engine 41's "Advanced" rig. Finally in 1998 they became Squad 41, converting from an Engine Company to Squad Company, just like Engines 18,61,252,270, and 288.

Now for all of you who may be totally baffled and befuddled as to what a squad is, it is the farthest thing from the famous Squad 51 of the TV series *EMERGENCY!* A squad company, or at least the FDNY's squad companies, are rescue-pumpers, meaning that they carry water and can pump it, but they also carry specialized rescue equipment like the Hurst Tool (the Jaws of Life), and other equipment that a ladder company would carry, like forcible entry tools. Members of Squad Companies also have special Hazardous Materials (Haz-Mat) training, and all the squad companies run special haz-mat support vans (see also Staten Island–Engine 160/Rescue 5/Division 8/TSU 2) for Haz-Mat emergencies, because it would be particularly cumbersome for Haz-Mat 1 (located in Queens, with ironically enough, Squad 288) to roll on every Haz-Mat response in the city. Squads also can operate as engine companies, ladder companies, or squads at fire scenes, it is up to the chief in charge as to which one they operate as. They also have positions from an engine company namely, the Officer, the M.P.O. (Motor Pump Operator, who also drives the rig sometimes known as the chauffeur), the Nozzle position (the member assigned to the hose line and on the front of it), the B.U. (Backup), the member assigned to Control or to the Standpipe, and the member assigned to the Door. Operating as a squad, they would be the officer, chauffeur, Irons (which is also a position on a ladder company), the member assigned to the Hook (for all of you who read books on firemen as kids, the hook is colloquial for the pike-pole), the Saw, and finally the member assigned to the Roof (also a position on a ladder company)

Like the rescue companies, one must request an interview with Squad 41's captain to become a member (same thing goes for Squads 1, 18, 61, 252, 270, and 288), and go through a probationary period on the company. And also like the rescue companies, it ultimately is up to the captain if the member stays with Squad 41.

Engine 41 also was a victim or participant, (I'm not sure which is the proper word for it, you be the judge) in the FDNY's experiment with chartreuse (a shade of lime green) painted rigs in the early '80s. During the late '70s, one of the fire engine manufacturerers who has since gone under, Ward LaFrance, and OSHA (Occupational Safety and Health Administration) led a charge for rigs to be painted chartreuse for visibility purposes. The FDNY experimented with it, and thus Engine 41 ran a chartreuse engine out of these quarters from 1981 onwards until about the time of their disbandment in 1989. The other companies who ran chartreuse rigs also ran red reserves or second pieces. The end result of the FDNY's experiment with chartreuse actually was a success, despite the fact that chartreuse rigs were problematic with the morale of the firefighters, and were involved in more traffic accidents than red rigs. The success was that all rigs after 1983 were painted red and white and given more lights to be more of a presence on city streets. At another time, during the tumultuous 70's, when they were Engine 41, they ran a Squad out of these quarters, the former Squad 5, which was their second piece (see Engine 72/Satellite 2). Worth a look-see!

Squad Company 61, Battalion 20
1518 Williamsbridge Road

Author has particularly detailed knowledge.

Another beautiful neighbor to Einstein Hospital, they are also near neighbors to the 49th Precinct. Battalion 20 is responsible for all of the Bronx between Co-op City and the Whitestone and Throgs Neck Bridges, including City Island, which is a total of nine companies, including the aforementioned Engines 70, 72, 89 and Ladders 50 and 53, and Satellite 2. The other companies in Battalion 20 which are not mentioned here are Engine 90 and Ladder 41, quartered on White Plains Road. Battalion 20 is the only battalion I can think of off the top of my head to run exclusively tower ladders. The firehouse again is a near twin to Engine 320/Ladder 167, and they are well worth your time and energy! Go visit em!

Time to establish some *POSSIBLE TRIPS:*

Engine 38/Ladder 51, Squad 61/Battalion 20, Engine 63/Battalion 15, Engine 66/Ladder 61, Engine 70/Ladder 53, Engine 72/Satellite 2, Engine 89/Ladder 50, and Engine 97. Those firehouses are all within a 2 to 3 mile radius of one another, and if you're up for walking, you can walk, or to get to City Island, take the BX12 or BX29 bus (**be sure to check current schedules/listings**). The #6 subway train stops at Buhre Avenue and at Westchester Square, and it's a short walk from either of those stations to Squad 61/Battalion 20, or to Engine 89/Ladder 50. To get to Engine 63/Battalion 15, I recommend you take the rush hours #5 subway train (denoted by a diamond on subway maps) to its end at Nereid Avenue or to 233rd Street Station. Heck, one could potentially visit all of the firehouses in the 15th Battalion (as we have done) in a few hours. The 15th

Battalion firehouses are again: Engine 38/Ladder 51, Engine 63/Battalion 15, Engine 66/Ladder 61, Engine 97, and Ladder 39. There is a 233rd Street crosstown bus, and the #2 train stops at 233rd Street right near Engine 63/Battalion 15's house. The #4 train also has its terminus at Woodlawn, right on Ladder 39's back door. The #5 train also makes stops near Engine 38/Ladder 51 and Engine 97, and there are many buses to and from Co-op City, just be careful about getting lost on Co-op City's streets (some of which are called Loops).

Those are all so close, you can make an entire day out of just those! There are many good places to eat and buy stuff, of note, The Chirping Chicken, on Buhre Avenue; also of note for the kid in your life, Steve's Pelham Bay Toy, at Westchester Avenue and Buhre. Be warned though if you are driving, there is an elevated subway (the #6) over Westchester Avenue., and I-95 in that area can have hellishly heavy traffic at certain times. And for all you who like chain stores, Co-op City has a lot!

Another trip is Squad 41, Engine 71/Ladder 55/Division 6, and a New York Yankees game. All of those firehouses are within a mile of Yankee Stadium. Security is an issue in those areas, less so during the day. Go enjoy the Bronx!

Engine 72/Satellite 2's quarters on East Tremont Avenue in the Bronx near the Cross Bronx Expressway. The pole shaft the large cylindrical column to the left of the appartus bay. Note also how the facade says "ENGINE 72 LADDER", as this firehouse was once Ladder 55's quarters. (Henry Schneiderman Photo)

Ladder 51's old tower ladder truck, taken after a drill session at Michealangelo Junior High School. The firefighters next to the truck are preparing to "take up", or leave the scene, having finished operations. This was the same Ladder 51 that I went up the bucket in. (Henry Schneiderman Photo)

6

MANHATTAN

"Hot town, Summer in the City,
Back of my neck gettin' dirt and gritty
Been down, isn't a pity,
Doesn't seem to be a shadow in the city.
All around, the people looking half-dead,
Walking on the sidewalk, hotter than a matchhead": the song
"Summer in the City", is a perfect description of Manhattan, and
what its like to be a firefighter there. Because Manhattan is so big
(actually it isn't, it's 13 miles long and 2 miles at its widest, it's just
really densely populated), we will split things up. Lower Manhattan runs from Battery Park and Bowling Green to 14th Street;
Midtown is 14th to 59th; Uptown is 59th upwards. So, let's get
started right at the bottom of things, really, I mean it!

Engine Company 4, Ladder Company 15, Decon Trailer (Decontamination)

42 South Street between Gouverneur Lane and Old Slip.

Featured in the *AIA Guide to New York City*, Third Edition,
Author knows particular firefighters here by name.

Although these guys FQ were mentioned in the Necrology section of the AIA guide, they now have a beautiful modern firehouse, built into the skyscraper in the back of 1 Financial Square. Ladder 15 has gotten around, and at one time they were housed with Engine 10 in another brother firehouse to Engine 320/Ladder 167 on Water Street, (the one the *AIA Guide* gave honorable mention to in the Necrology), and one time, believe it or not, they were quartered with Engine 38 in uptown Manhattan way back when! Engine 4 has also gotten around in its own way, they've been disbanded, reinstated, etc, but they've been in the same part of Manhattan these many years, first on Maiden Lane and then in the Water Street Firehouse, and finally this modern piece of work! This firehouse is now responsible for most or all the responses in the Financial District and any at Battery Park or on Wall Street. This firehouse also protects Trinity Church (the foot of Wall Street at Broadway). Both companies also have nifty logo, specifically, a bull with the street sign for Wall Street in its mouth, in a rage, charging. Even though they are technically located south of Wall Street (Gouverneur Lane is the next block south of Wall Street), the Battalion 1 patch (of which they are a part) says next to them "WALL STREET", but their official mottos are the "Fabulous Four" (Engine 4) and the "Wall Street Bulls" (Ladder 15). On my last visit, a plaque had already been placed at their firehouse commemorating the twelve firefighters from their firehouse who died on September 11th. Furthermore, the firehouse is so large that many companies could be relocated here if necessary. I also met a nice guy who was detailed there from Ladder 20, Kevin. Also on my last visit, Engine 4 was running a Mack CF spare that was in current FDNY colors, as opposed to the red and white of past years, which most spares are still painted. These guys are one of the southernmost if not the southernmost firehouse in the borough of Manhattan. Go visit 'em!

Engine Company 6
49 Beekman Street

Author has particularly detailed knowledge thanks to kind tour by firefighters. Author knows particular firefighter(s) here by name.

The "Tigers", called such because in the 19th century their rig had a painting of a tiger on it, they are right across the street from the Beekman–Downtown Division of NYU Medical Centers, are within walking distance of City Hall, and are literally right at the street approaches to the Brooklyn Bridge!

Speaking of the 19th Century, when this company was still a volunteer company, their foreman at one time (the 19th century equivalent to the rank of captain) was William "Boss" Tweed! "Boss" Tweed evidently was also behind some other volunteer fire companies, and the racketeers of that era evidently had a fair amount of influence on the volunteer companies (who were rivals at the time), and many foremen of that era evidently were easily corrupted. *The Encyclopedia of New York City* talks more about "Boss" Tweed and the volunteer rivalry (see also For Further Reference "A"). This company has always protected that area of Lower Manhattan, starting off further south near what is now Nassau Street, and eventually moving north to their current quarters on Beekman Street. Their firehouse is like many of its kind, sandwiched between larger buildings, and I wonder why these guys weren't mentioned in the *AIA Guide*, given that the firm that constructed their firehouse, Horgan and Slattery, gets mentioned a great deal and also is responsible for several other firehouses in the city. This firehouse also is a little bit of a twin to Engine 23's house uptown, even though Horgan and Slattery weren't the architects of Engine 23's quarters. This firehouse was also the quarters of Engine 32 but when Engine 6's quarters on Liberty Street (see also Manhattan Engine 10/Ladder 10) were torn down in 1970, Engine 6 moved in and Engine 32 was ultimately disbanded in 1972. The address, 49 Beekman Street, has also seemingly always been a municipal facility of some sort, first the 2nd Precinct of the NYPD, then this majestic firehouse. The firehouse has also housed Engine 7 and many other companies. It is also one of the twelve firehouses that I have visited without my Dad. A short walk from City Hall, Wall Street, or from the Brooklyn Bridge (one website lists their neighborhood as "Brooklyn Bridge", they are that close!), they are a superb visit.

Engine Company 10, Ladder Company 10
124 Liberty Street

This firehouse was in the shadow of the south tower of the World Trade Center before the September 11th terrorist attacks which brought both towers down. On September 11th itself, this firehouse became a command post where firefighters went for equipment, and continues to serve as such in the clean-up operations there. Before September 11th, this firehouse was known as "The Ten House", and firefighters from the house often helped tourists visiting the World Trade Center or the Financial District. I visited this house a month before that fateful day (August 4, 2001). The firehouse presently is in need of heavy repair, and thus Ladder 10 is quartered with Engine 4/Ladder 15 on South Street, and Engine 10 is quartered on Duane Street with Engine 7/Ladder 1/Battalion 1 temporarily. Both firehouses though are large enough to handle those rigs being located there. Before both companies united there in 1984, Engine 10 had been located across town with Ladder 15, as aforementioned, and Ladder 10 had been quartered with the now disbanded Engine 29 on Fulton Street near Vesey Street, and in the great budget crunch of the 70's, Ladder 10 was disbanded. Engine 29 is also where Ed Schneider of the book *A Fire Chief Remembers* (see also For Further Reference "A") was assigned as a lieutenant shortly after his promotion to that rank in 1939. Ironically enough, in the construction of the World Trade Center, a firehouse down the street from them (113 Liberty) was demolished, the FQ of Engine 6.

Ladder 10's current rig actually is a unique one, it is a 2002 Seagrave 100' aerial, but it has a mural on the side of it with a portrait of one of the firefighters raising the flag over ground zero, and the American Flag on it, which I saw in person on my visit to Engine 4/Ladder 15 on June 7, 2002. On a weirder note, Engine 10 was also a participant or victim (you be the judge) of the FDNY's experiment with chartreuse. Engine 10's motto also changed a bit in the wake of the September 11th terrorist attacks, its motto has now become "Protecting Liberty", which makes sense, given their location on Liberty Street.

If you wish to see this firehouse, you can go to a viewing platform at the World Trade Center site, and if you are looking west, it will be on your left. Or you can simply walk along Church Street or West Street (if you can, check to see if Church Street isn't closed off still) down to the World Trade Center site, and if you look along Liberty Street, you will definitely spot their house. Once cleanup and reconstruction is completed there, they will be a great visit!

Engine Company 7, Ladder Company 1, Battalion 1
100 Duane Street between Broadway/Church Street

Featured in the *AIA Guide to New York City*, Third Edition, Author knows particular firefighters here by name, Author has particularly detailed knowledge.

This firehouse is another triple crown winner! Situated a few blocks north of City Hall, it is a beautiful firehouse with a lot of history to it. This firehouse was once the Fire Museum, and also served as an infirmary when a fire broke out way back when at one of the firehouse's neighbors on Duane Street. This firehouse also carries the unique honor of being the 50th firehouse I have visited!

Engine 7 has a very long history, dating back to September 8th, 1865. Engine 7 has always been in the vicinity of City Hall, first on Chambers Street, later on Centre Street, and finally in this house on Duane Street. At one time they were assigned a second piece, and they have always been quartered with Ladder 1. Ladder 1 carries a very high honor: they are the oldest fire company in the city. They were initially organized as a volunteer company before the Revolutionary War, circa 1774 or so, and have been service since then, becoming a paid company on the same date as Engine 7. Ladder 1 also marked the city's first foray into tower ladders in 1964, (a tower ladder is a ladder truck with a bucket on the end and with a ladder on the mechanism to send the ladder up), and has remained a tower ladder ever since. The first tower ladder actually was a standard issue Mack C fire engine with the tower ladder mechanism (the boom and bucket and hoses and pipes) designed and built by two companies, Baker-Aerialscope and Truco, and for years Ladder 1 was the city's only tower ladder. That foray resulted in nearly half of the department's ladder companies becoming tower ladders from tiller ladders or aerial ladders. In fact, Ladder 1 calls themselves "The Original One" (referring to the fact that they were the first tower ladder) on their patches. Probably the only other tower ladder that has a history like Ladder 1's is Ladder 119 in Brooklyn, but that's only because they had a similar rig when the department converted them to tower ladders in the 60's.

This firehouse is responsible for a large part of Downtown Manhattan, including City Hall, parts of the Financial District, and the former World Trade Center. In fact, one of Engine 7's patches over the years had the twin towers of the World Trade Center on it. This firehouse also was the subject of the famous documentary "9-11", made by two French brothers, Jules and Gedeon Naudet, who originally intended to follow a probationary firefighter or Probie, (FDNY colloquial for a rookie firefighter), Tony Benetatos, as he became a member of the fire department and a brother in battle. The brothers had a friend who was a member of Ladder 1, Firefighter James Hanlon, so when Tony was assigned to that house, it became easy to follow him. On the evening of September 10th, the Jules and Gedeon had cooked the men of the firehouse a meal, and on the morning of September 11th, at about 8:40, Engine 7, Ladder 1, Battalion 1, and Ladder 8 received a call for a gas leak. Jules rode with Battalion Chief Joseph Pfeifer out to the gas leak. Upon their arrival, while Chief Pfeifer was getting a gas meter out of his Battalion Chief's Suburban, the firefighters and the Jules heard a plane flying very low, and when Jules turned his camera up towards the plane, he caught the only known footage of the first plane crashing into the north tower of the World Trade Center. Battalion Chief Pfeifer and his men immediately left the gas leak and transmitted a third alarm for the north tower of the World Trade Center, or box 8087. Anyway, Jules followed Battalion Chief Pfeifer and his aide into the lobby of the World Trade Center and stayed with him at the command post he set up. Jules got the only footage of the inside of the World Trade Center on that horrible day, and actually saved some lives that day when the south tower collapsed. When the south tower collapsed, all the dust and smoke flowed straight into the lobby of the north tower (the windows had been blown out when the plane hit), and it became impossible to see in the lobby of north tower, and his camera light became a searchlight to help Chief Pfeifer and the other firefighters trapped there get out just minutes before the north tower collapsed. While both companies lost their rigs that day (Engine 7's has since been replaced, I'll talk more about it shortly), none of the men of Engine 7, Ladder 1, nor Chief Pfeifer and his aide, nor did Jules or Gedeon, but some twenty men from the other firehouses in their battalion died. Jules and Gedeon also followed the first days of the cleanup and recovery at the World Trade Center.

I finally visited that house on June 5, 2002, after reading about it for 10 years and seeing "9-11". On my visit, the firehouse was undergoing some renovation, but none specifically in the apparatus bay. I met a firefighter named Mark then, and saw Engine 7's new rig, and Engine 10's new rig. I never saw Ladder 1's rig (they had a run when I was visiting), but I did get to see a good deal of the inside of the firehouse. This firehouse actually has the street sign for Duane Street on the inside, and is very very large. The engine and ladder fit into one large garage area with two separate bays, and the chief's vehicle fits between the two, and there is another entire apparatus bay, where Engine 10 currently resides, and could house another company or Battalion 1. This firehouse also has a neon sign with Engine 7, Ladder 1 and Battalion 1 on it. Battalion 1's responsibility is all of Manhattan from Battery Park north to City Hall on the east side, and parts of TriBeCa (Triangle Below Canal, referring to Canal Street) on the west side, including the Financial District, Manhattan sides of the Brooklyn and Manhattan Bridges, Hanover Square, Battery Park City, and the World Financial Center, just to name a few neighborhoods and key places. Battalion 1 also has been quartered with all of the present companies within it, in fact for many years it was quartered with Ladder 10, and before moving in with Engine 7 and Ladder 1, Ladder 15. Engine 7 also has a nifty motto, namely "The Magnificent Seven Engine". This firehouse is probably one of the best visits in the city! Go visit "The Magnificent Seven Engine," and "The First Tower Ladder", you'll have a great time, just as I did!

Ladder Company 8
14 North Moore Street at Varick Street

Author knows firefighters here by name, author has particularly detailed knowledge.

This firehouse, despite being a small one situated on a relatively quiet corner in TriBeCa, has a great deal of fame associated with it. It is the famous "Ghostbusters Firehouse", where the movie "Ghostbusters" was filmed. At present, it is a landmark firehouse, home to a quiet ladder company. On my visit there on June 5, 2002, many little things associated with Ghostbusters were in that firehouse, one of which was a large "Ghostbusters" logo hanging on the wall in the appartus bay. Additionally, I saw a montage of photos taken when "Ghostbusters" was filmed at the firehouse sitting on the wall. It is probably one of the most famous firehouses in the City of New York, possibly one the most famous firehouse from New York in the world. On another historical note, Ladder 8 was once quartered in the firehouse which is now the FDNY Fire Museum on Spring Street (which you'll see a little later).

Presently, Ladder 8 is responsible for the neighborhood known as TriBeCa, which includes some nice architecture and is also responsible for parts of SoHo. Although they only get about 1200 runs per year, the city keeps them over there for aerial ladder protection for the 2nd Battalion and for TriBeCa, the Lower West Side, and some parts of Downtown Manhattan near City Hall, given that the other Ladder Company near them, Ladder 1, runs a tower ladder. This firehouse also was one of the first to respond to the World Trade Center on September 11th, and subsequently lost their rig in the collapse, but had a new rig delivered on September 14th, which I saw on my visit. I also met a kind veteran of the department there, a Firefighter Dinkins, who has spent 17 and 1/2 years at Ladder 8. Go visit the "Land of the Loft", it's a great visit in TriBeCa!

Ladder Company 20, Medical Division, Division I
253 Lafayette Street, between Prince and Spring Street

Author has particularly detailed knowledge thanks to kind tours by fire-fighters.

These guys, also the temporary quarters of Squad 18, were at one time quarters to Engine 13. At present, they are a very large and modern firehouse, with the unusual feature of a bay in a position similar to that of a normal garage, below ground level. The medical division is where firefighters go to rehabilitate after injuries. Ladder 20 calls themselves "SoHo Trucking Company", and they run a tiller ladder truck, which is slowly becoming an antiquated idea as a fire engine (no offense to the men of Ladder 20 or any of the 12 remaining tiller ladders in the city!) Ladder 20's FQ on Mercer Street actually is particularly famous; at one time it was the "Fireman's Hall", which back in the days of volunteers, was where the firefighters used to congregate, and when the paid depart-ment came about in 1865, it became Ladder 20's quarters. That house was also featured in the *AIA Guide*, as was Engine 13's FQ. Ironically, the now disbanded <u>ENGINE</u> 20 was the same site that Ladder 20 occupies now (Lafayette between Spring and Prince). Division 1 is responsible for all responses between Battery Park and 34th Street, which includes Greenwich Village, the Empire State Building, the Chelsea Piers, Union Square, Penn Station, and the Financial District, just to name a few areas. Ladder 20 also carries a very unique honor in the history of my buffing in New York City and total; they are the only firehouse in New York City (and one of two total) where I have met a Dalmatian. On my brief visit on December 28th, 2001, a little Dalmatian puppy, whose name I have since forgotten, was there, wagging his tail and being a good dog. They are also almost next-door neighbors to the Fire Store, which sells everything and anything FDNY-related. T-Shirts, patches, you name it! They also have another store that sells stuff relating to NYPD, Corrections and other city agencies, called The Police Shop. The Fire Store by the way is open from 10AM-6PM Monday-Saturday. Go visit all three!

Engine Company 33, Ladder Company 9
42-44 Great Jones Street

Author has particularly detailed knowledge thanks to kind tours by fire-fighters. Featured in the *AIA Guide to New York City*, Third Edition.

One of the most beautiful firehouses in the city, it has a glorious history. Built in 1898, it was the fire chief's personal headquarters at one time. It is where Rescue Company 1 got its beginning on March 8, 1915 at 0800 hours, running a specially modified Cadillac Touring Car. The architect who designed it at the turn of the century, Ernest Flagg, is also known for a firehouse in far uptown Manhattan, namely Engine 67's quarters. Ernest Flagg is perhaps best known for some of his civilian architecture, mainly in Lower Manhattan, SoHo, and the Villages. Right now the firehouse is known as the "Bowery U", and although it doesn't protect Greenwich Village, it provides fire protection to the East Village, New York University (NYU, whose Web site mentions them) and Astor Place. Ladder 9 also runs one of two 95 foot tower ladders in Division 1 and was also seen briefly in the documentary "Brothers in Battle". This firehouse also is one my dad's favorites in the city, if not his favorite over all. Go visit the "Bowery U"!

Engine Company 55
363 Broome Street

Featured in the *AIA Guide to New York City*, Third Edition.

"Cinquentecinque" as they are known from the Italian words for "fifty-five", protects Little Italy and some of Chinatown. They are a beautiful little firehouse, akin to many others in the city. They also have rather patriotic coloring, namely red, white and blue. This firehouse was also the F.Q. of Battalion 2 who has since been moved across town to Engine 24/Ladder 5's quarters on 6th Avenue. This firehouse also has a nifty patch, namely a firefighter on a flying horse flying over Little Italy with a hook (more commonly known to civilians as the pike-pole), ready to extinguish fires. My mother, upon seeing that patch for sale on Eagleemblems.com, purchased it in a New York Minute! Go visit them and see Little Italy's protection!

Ladder Company 3, Battalion 6
108 East 13th Street, between 4th/3rd.

Although these guys are on the brink of being in Midtown, they still are downtown because they're on 13th Street (No offense to any members of either company who reads it!). Ironically enough, this company was organized on September 11th, 1865. It has apparently always been on 108 E. 13th, but has been through two firehouses. Their present house was built in 1929. These guys protect Union Square and that eastern part of Manhattan, and they still have the sign of the FQ of Water Tower 2, across the top of their firehouse. Ladder 3 calls themselves "Recon", and the 6th Battalion's slogan is "From the Bowery to Bellevue". Go visit them!

Before we go to Midtown, there is another former firehouse worth mention, and I have to talk about the Fire Museum.

(FQ) Engine Company 31, Battalion 2, Water Tower 3
87 Lafayette Street

Featured in the *AIA Guide to New York City*, Third Edition.

Presently the home of a video production company, this could easily be mistaken for a chateau somewhere in Montpellier or Nice! Although graffiti has detracted from its beauty in some ways, it still is a wonderfully majestic former firehouse. For anyone who's wondering, the Water Tower was the turn of the century (19th to 20th) equivalent of a tower ladder today, except without a bucket on the end for firefighters to operate. It was just a very high boom with a nozzle on the end. *Fire Engines in North America* (see For Further Reference "A") by Sheila Buff talks a great deal about water towers, with an entire chapter called "Chemical Wagons, Aerials, and Water Towers". The book *Services Not Required* (see also Brooklyn-Engine 207/Ladder 110/Satellite 6/FCU 1 and 2/Battalion 31/Division 11) also discussed water towers. There actually is a famous photo of a water tower being tested at this very firehouse, which actually is the cover art on *Services Not Required*, and also seen in *Fire Engines in North America*. Go visit!

(FQ) Engine Company 30, Battalion 5, Rescue Company 1, now New York City Fire Museum
278 Spring Street

Featured in the *AIA Guide to New York City*, Third Edition.

This firehouse was once the only triple combination firehouse in the city way back when (Engine 30 ran three separate rigs). Now it is home to New York City's Fire Museum. The Fire museum has a bit of its own history. The Fire Museum began at the famous "Duane Street Firehouse" in Downtown Manhattan (now the quarters of Engine 7/Ladder 1/Battalion 1), but when that firehouse became used again for current rigs and firefighting, the museum needed a new home, and so they moved into this majestic firehouse in TriBeCa. Of note at this museum is an old searchlight truck (remember, we were talking about searchlight rigs at the Jay Street firehouse), specifically an old 1959 Mack, which was still in service in the 1970's (despite the budget crunch!!!!). This searchlight was Searchlight 21. and the fact that this museum is very very kid friendly. Heck, you can have birthday parties there! A wonderful visit for the fire historian or for the kid in you or for the architectural historian.

Engine 4/Ladder 15/Decon Trailer's quarters on South Street in the Financial District. This firehouse, as aforementioned, is built the back of 1 Financial Square, a high-rise building between Gouveur-neur Lane, Old Slip, Front Street, and South Street. Ironically, in the construction of 1 Financial Square and the other high-rises in that area, Engine 4/Ladder 15's FQ on Water Street was demolished. This firehouse's next door neighbor is, ironically enough, a former police precinct (the 1st), now the Police Museum. (Joseph Schneiderman Photo)

The plaque commemerating the 14 firefighters from Engine 4 and Ladder 15 who were killed on September 11th, 2001 at the World Trade Center. This photo was taken on June 7th, 2002, less the one year after the terrorist attacks on the World Trade Center. It is customary in the FDNY to place plaques at the firehouses were firefighters have died in the line of duty, but those plaques can take nearly a year to actually be placed. Not the case here. (Joseph Schneiderman Photo)

Engine 6's quarters on Beekman Street near City Hall. This firehouse was once home to Engine 32, and as you can see, the #6's placed there were placed over the original numbers 32. If you look closely on the left side of the firehouse, you can see two Maltese crosses that say "F.D." in the top, "6" in the middle, and "N.Y." on the bottom. Finally, you can also see a small logo on the same side of the firehouse that says "ENGINE COMPANY 6" and beneath that, "TIGERS". (Joseph Schneiderman Photo)

The famous "Ten House", or Engine 10/Ladder 10's quarters on Liberty Street immediatly behind the World Trade Center. My dad, Henry Schneiderman, can be seen in front of the apparatus bay, and a firefighter can be seen directing tourists towards Greenwich Street. This photo was taken some four years before the events of September 11th, 2001. (Photo Courtesy of Henry Schneiderman)

Ladder 10's old 1994 Seagrave 100' aerial ladder, driving east on Liberty Street towards their quarters in the shadow of the south tower of the World Trade Center. This photo was taken on August 4, 2001, barely a month before the Septmber 11th, 2001 terrorist attacks that destroyed the World Trade Center, and is last photo I have of anything related to that firehouse before September 11th. It is further significant because that rig was also destroyed on September 11th. (Joseph Schneiderman Photo)

Engine 7's 2002 Seagrave Pumper, taken in their quarters on Duane Street. This firehouse,the subject of a documentary originally intended to follow a probationary firefighter through his rise through the ranks, later followed the horror of September 11th as it unfolded, although it lost no men, lost all three of their rigs (Ladder 1 is also quartered here, as is Battalion 1) that fateful day. By the time this photo was taken (June 5th, 2002), Engine 7's rig had already been replaced. Note the American Flag, and Engine 7's logo on the area on passenger cars normally called the B-pillar (the area between the doors). (Joseph Schneiderman Photo)

MANHATTAN | **79**

Battalion 1's Chevrolet Suburban, also taken in their quarters on Duane Street. Battalion Chiefs at one time had had Chrysler K-Cars as their means of getting around, but after a fatal accident involving such a vehicle, Battalion Chiefs were assigned diesel-powered Chevrolet or GMC Suburbans, and recently, Ford Excursions. The reason why they are diesel-powered is because the fire engines are powered by diesel fuel, and is it more feasible to have a vehicle powered by diesel as opposed to gasoline. (Joseph Schneiderman Photo)

Ladder 8's quarters on North Moore Street in TriBeCa. This fire-house was the base of operations in the movie "Ghostbusters". This firehouse is right on the corner of Varick Street (most firehouses are inward of major streets), and is right across from the current First Precinct of the NYPD on Ericson Place. (Joseph Schneiderman Photo)

A frontal shot of Ladder 8's aerial ladder truck, taken in their quarters on North Moore Street. This rig, a 2001 Seagrave, was delivered, ironically enough on September 14th, 2001, days after Ladder 8 had lost their previous rig at the World Trade Center. All fire engines have white reflective tape on them, which explains the near halos on certain parts of the rig. (Joseph Schneiderman Photo)

Ladder 20/Medical Division/Division 1's quarters on Lafayette Street in the SoHo (South of Houston) neighborhood of Manhattan. This firehouse currently occupies the site of the now disbanded ENGINE 20's quarters. This firehouse was also home to Engine 13 before their disbandment in the budget crunch of the 70's, and currently is (or was, buffs check me) Squad 18's temporary quarters while their quarters on 10th Street are renovated. This firehouse also is the Manhattan Arson Unit's headquarters. (Joseph Schneiderman Photo)

Engine 33/Ladder 9's quarters on Great Jones Street in the East Village. Note how many stories high the firehouse is and the arch above the appartus bay, and the deck immeaditly behind the American Flag. Although you can't see it, the facade above the appartus bay does NOT say "Engine Co. 33,Ladder Co.9", or something along those lines, rather it simply says "33 ENGINE COMPANY 33" in the style that was common in the old FDNY. It is fairly easy to see why this firehouse was featured in the *AIA Guide to New York City*. (Henry Schneiderman Photo)

Engine 55's quarters in Little Italy on Broome Street. The firehouse was also featured in the *AIA Guide to New York City*. The patriotic coloring is easy to see in the facade area in and around the appartus bay, especially with the lettering denoting that the firehouse is Engine 55's quarters. The metalwork done immeaditly above the appartus bay is similar to that of a cathedral, and note the gargoyle perched above the firehouse, seemingly perfectly placed. (Henry Schneiderman Photo)

Time to go to Midtown! Again, we start at the south end of Midtown.

Engine Company 5
340 East 14th Street, between 1st/2nd Avenue

This firehouse just makes into Midtown by being on 14th Street itself! It is actually the only firehouse in Manhattan located on 14th Street, and I believe the only one in Manhattan on a major crosstown thoroughfare aside from Engine 9/Ladder 6's location on Canal Street, Engine 36's location on 125th Street in Ladder 14's FQ and Engine 37/Ladder 40, also located on 125th Street, but on the other side (I don't know of any active firehouses on Chambers Street, Houston Street, 8th Street, 23rd Street, 34th Street, 42nd Street, or 57th Street, just to name a couple of the big crosstown thoroughfares). There are, ironically enough, firehouses on 43rd Street (two!!!, one of which we'll see), and 58th Street (which we'll see also), and finally, we also know of Ladder 3's quarters on 13TH STREET. Engine 5 dates back to the department's paid beginnings in 1865 (at least!), and except for a brief 6 months in 1880-1881 and an equally brief period between 1998-1999, they have always been quartered at 340 East 14th Street. This firehouse is responsible for the Stuyvesant Town housing and the Peter Cooper housing, and actually a significant portion of eastern Manhattan, given that the next firehouse north on their "side" of Manhattan is Engine 16/Ladder 7 (on 29th Street!!) and the next one south is Engine 28/Ladder 11 (on 2nd Street!!), both of which are in different battalions (4 and 8 respectively), where as Engine 5 is in, ironically enough, Battalion 6. Engine 5 also runs the only Foam unit below 125th Street in Manhattan, designated of course, Foam 5 (in the FDNY, foam units are always designated after the engine company quartered with them). I wonder actually why this company isn't busy, given that they do run the only Foam unit from Battery Park all the way up to 125th Street. Then again, there probably aren't that many responses that would call for Foam 5, given that there aren't large oil containers or an airport nearby (where foam is the preferred method of firefighting, and in Brooklyn where there are such areas, there are a truckload of foam units). Engine 5's firehouse also is an old beauty, having been featured in some paintings, has some luxurious woodwork around the number "5" on the sides of the facade of the firehouse, almost like something royal or Victorian. The firehouse is also one of the last firehouses to still have the FDNY's preferred font from it's early paid days continuing into the 1940's or so for the lettering on its facade, which is some derivative of the "Old West" font (seen on those "WANTED" signs). The same part of the firehouse where the facade is painted some shade of Fire Engine Red, with the rest of the firehouse in brick. Like many of its' kind (and like the kind I've been jabbering on about for this entire book, solo companies), it is sandwiched between buildings, but with the building on its west side is a florist. Situated on the convergence of Downtown and Midtown, it is a beautiful little house, protecting a nice tenement. Go visit the "14th Street Express", and maybe you'll add your name to the list of people who have painted it, and be able to brag to your friends and fellow buffs (I personally didn't) that you visited Engine 5 AND Foam 5!

Engine Company 14
14 East 18th Street

One of Union Square's firehouses, they are a beautiful piece of architecture. When I visited this station, it was around the holidays, and the firehouse blended right in with the decoration. One reason why the decorations blended is because some of the exterior decoration is green, possibly engraved holly or laurel. This firehouse also has "F.D.N.Y." painted on the garage door panels. Go see this little piece of art!

Engine Company 3, Ladder Company 12, 7th Battalion
146 West 19th Street, between 6th/7th Avenue

Author knows particular firefighter(s) here by name.

"The Pride of Chelsea", this house protects the west side of Manhattan, specifically, the Chelsea neighborhood just above Greenwich Village. They are evidently a busy house, as when I stopped by, the engine and ladder were both out. Ladder 12 carries the unusual honor of being the last of the original 12 paid ladder companies to be organized. Additionally, Ladder 12 is the other 95 foot tower ladder in Division 1. (To all the buffs out there or people who are just plain confused, given that I've been talking about 95 foot tower ladders for a while, you can pick a Seagrave one out by looking at its wheels. If the wheels are silver, than it's a 95 footer. Mack 95-footers also typically have 4 doors as opposed to the two that 75 footers have.) The 7th Battalion also is a relatively large battalion, protecting the Chelsea Piers, Penn Station, the Empire State Building, and Hell's Kitchen. They also protect certain northern parts of Greenwich Village and that region near and along 14th Street. The firehouse, in terms of architecture, is a near twin to Engine 22/Ladder 13/Battalion 10 uptown. Go visit "The Pride of Chelsea"!

Engine Company 1, Ladder Company 24
146 West 31st Street, between 6th/7th Avenue

This firehouse is visible from Penn Station, its neighbor to the north and west, and in addition to protecting Penn Station, they also protect the Empire State Building and Madison Square Garden. Their firehouse is somewhat old, and the firehouse is also the former quarters of Division 3, although now Division 3 is quartered with Ladder 25 uptown. Engine 1 was the first paid company organized, on July 31st, 1865, at 4 Centre Street, very close to City Hall. When the FDNY celebrated their 125th Anniversary in 1990, Engine 1 also celebrated its 125th anniversary as the oldest engine company (remember that LADDER 1 is the oldest company of any kind the city.) This firehouse's motto is "Midtown Madness", which makes sense, given that they are in the heart of Midtown with all the big sites insanely close by! A grand visit, good to combine with the Empire State Building or anything else in Midtown!

Rescue Company I
530 West 43rd Street

Featured in the *AIA Guide to New York City*, Third Edition. Author has particularly detailed knowledge.

A modern little firehouse, sandwiched in Hell's Kitchen, only a few blocks from the *U.S.S. Intrepid* and the Circle Line, they are Manhattan's Rescue Company. In order to be on Rescue 1, a firefighter must request an interview with Rescue 1's captain, and go through a probationary period on the company. The same holds true for the other four rescue companies, as aforementioned with Rescue 4. Although 3 of the 5 rescue companies are quartered alone (meaning no other companies are stationed in the house with them), Rescue 1's quarters are the only ones designed exclusively for a rescue company. Rescue 2 in Brooklyn has the former quarters of Engine 234 and Salvage Company 1, and Rescue 3 in the Bronx has Engine 46's former quarters.

There have been extensive documentaries made exclusively about Rescue 1. Rescue 1 has also been featured on such programs like *48 Hours,* and *Rescue 911*. Also when their new rig was delivered on April 11, 2002, the *CBS Evening News* briefly featured them.

There is actually an ironic story behind Rescue 1's quarters, which I will tell. The site (530 West 43rd) had been home to Engine Company 2, but in the great budget cuts of the 1970s, Engine 2 fell victim to the vile 9 letter word: "Disbanded" (after 107 years of service). Rescue 1 thus moved in 1972, as previously they had been stationed at Engine 65, further east on 43rd Street, near Times Square. Before that, they'd been quartered at Engine 20's FQ on Lafayette Street, and before that, they were quartered with Engine 30 and Battalion 5 on Spring Street in the firehouse which is now the Fire Museum, and before that, they were organized with Engine 33 and Ladder 9 on Great Jones Street. On January 23rd, 1985, a 10th Alarm fire (or in FDNY lingo, a Borough Call) broke out at Rescue 1's neighbor, a large warehouse. Rescue 1 was at another response at the time. Two tower ladders had been set up to protect Rescue 1's quarters, but the warehouse eventually collapsed on top of Rescue 1's quarters, destroying the firehouse. The only thing left was the garage door, with Rescue 1's logo, the eagle. For that night, Rescue 1 moved in with Engine 23, but for the next four years until a new firehouse was built, they were quartered with Engine 34/Ladder 21 on 38th Street. The city actually was forced to take measures to prevent such an event from happening again. At the time, Ladders 4, 21 and 24 had all been aerial ladders, and Ladder 12 was the only tower ladder on the West Side (Ladder 7 is another tower ladder in Midtown, but on the East Side) at the time. Anyway, the city ultimately converted Ladder 21 to a tower ladder. Finally, in 1989, a new firehouse, designed with input from the firefighters, was completed at 530 West 43rd Street, and Rescue 1 returned to their quarters there. The aforementioned door was restored and placed in the back of the new firehouse, making an attraction to buffs everywhere. The *AIA Guide* actually has a very funny reference to them, "A substitute for-can you believe it, a firehouse that burned down?" (see also For Further Reference "A"). If you want to see what the old firehouse looked like, there are pictures of it on the FDNY's official website (see For Further Reference "B"). But if you want to see the door, you can be a slackjaw and visit their official website (see also For Further Reference "B") or visit them in person! They are worth a visit, but you may not catch them because they are so busy, given that Rescue 1 is responsible for all working fires (in FDNY radio code, a 10-75) in Manhattan between Battery Park and 110th Street on the West Side and 125th Street on the East Side, which is a total of 10 battalions and 2 divisions! If you are lucky enough to visit, and they don't have a run, you will see one of the more interesting rigs in FDNY history, a 2002 E-One (Emergency One)/Airbus Saulsbury Rescue Truck. That rig was designed, or based on the design plans of the late Captain Terry Hatton of Rescue 1 after looking through the designs of old rescue trucks (and having served on Rescue 2 and Rescue 1 for the majority of his career, that was what firefighters did to become members of Rescue 1, they served on Rescue 2 first, or at least he did), and seeing what worked in terms of design and what firefighters liked. Sadly, Captain Terry Hatton was one of 11, yes, 11 members from Rescue 1 who died on September 11th. However, after Rescue 1's rig was destroyed at the World Trade

Center, thanks to a special donation by Airbus based on Captain Terry Hatton's specifications, his dream of the ultimate rescue truck was posthumously realized. The rig is very long (some have said 34 feet)and was prominently featured in the news (as we talked about), and many of the FDNY photography websites had special sections devoted just to that truck. The rig also bears a red, white and blue miniature flag logo that says "Rescue 1" on it, and "Sept. 11, 2001", with the two towers of the World Trade Center representing the number 11. Finally, on the front of the rig, it carries Captain Hatton's motto, or common phrase (I honestly never figured out which one), "OUTSTANDING". On another note, Rescue 2 also runs a similar rig in Brooklyn, and a similar spare rescue truck is run out of S.O.C. (Special Operations Command) Headquarters on Roosevelt Island, and the other rescue companies are supposed to receive similar replacements soon. Like we've said, it is tough to visit Rescue 1 on account of their high amount of runs and large response area, but just visit, if nothing else, to see that rig. We personally have batted 0-for-4 on pass-bys.

Engine Company 8, Ladder Company 2, 8th Battalion
165 East 51st Street

Author knows particular firefighter(s) here by name.

Built into a high-rise building, these companies have a police precinct neighbor, the 17th, and protect much of Midtown including a stretch of Park Avenue. Both companies were organized on, ironically enough, September 11, 1865. The 8th Battalion calls itself "The High-Rise Capital of the World", and that is very true. After all, they are built into a high-rise building, and there are many high-rise buildings in and around where they are. The 8th Battalion also is responsible for a major part of Manhattan, pretty much everything on the East Side (and a little bit of the West Side) above 23rd Street, including the U.N., Grammercy Park, and the original Madison Square (23rd Street at Broadway and 5th Avenue). The little bit of the West Side I'm referring to is the area near Times Square. We'll talk a bit more about it at our next house. Battalion 8 also was the second busiest battalion in the city for several years, beating out battalions in Brownsville and Morrisania to name some of the harder hit areas. Engine 8 and Ladder 2 simply call themselves "Midtown Hi-Rise". Ladder 2 has Snoopy as its mascot. I believe this was because Snoopy is the mascot of MetLife, and the MetLife building towers over the neighborhood. Go visit these guys, it'll be some of the best fun you've had.

Before we continue, this next firehouse probably deserves its own chapter given that I know so much about it, and that it is one of my favorites, but it doesn't have one. Oh well. I guess I don't want to offend anyone over certain firehouses getting priority misconstrued as favoritism. So please, bear with me, as this firehouse gets a very long description, longer than that of Rescue 1, Engine 207/Ladder 110/Satellite 6/ Battalion 31/Division 11 and Engine 72/Satellite 2 combined.

Engine Company 54, Ladder Company 4, Battalion 9
782 Eighth Avenue at 48th Street

Featured in the *AIA Guide to New York City,* Third Edition. Author knows particular firefighter(s) here by name. Author has particularly detailed knowledge.

A triple-crown winner. I've been to this firehouse more times than any other in the city. I went on New Year's Eve 1996, April of 1998, December of 1998, August of 2001, December 28th, 2001, and March 15th, 2002. They were 1996's busiest fire station in NYC, and Ladder 4 was 1999's busiest ladder company. Their location is very central, it is a short walk to Times Square or Columbus Circle. Their mottoes are "Never Missed a Performance" and "Pride of Midtown". They are also a very unique company. Engine 54 is a "high-pressure" pumper, meaning that it is specially equipped to handle fires in high-rise buildings. Ladder 4 used to run the highest aerial ladder in Manhattan, a 110-footer, one of only five such "high-ladders" (110 foot aerial ladders), in New York City, and the only one in Manhattan. The high-ladders were phased out in 2001. Engine 54 was originally quartered on 47th Street, and I believe their former quarters still stands, as a Puerto Rican theater. Ironically enough, their old firehouse is a twin to Engine 53's old firehouse on 104th Street in Harlem, evidently designed by the same architectural firm. Ladder 4 has always been on the corner of 8th and 48th. Battalion 9 has gone back and forth over the years, but finally in 1974, all three companies united in a modern cubist firehouse. Battalion 9 also has been the busiest battalion in the city for several years in terms of runs and workers, and ironically enough Battalion 8 is second to them, as aforementioned! Battalion 9's response area is particularly diverse, namely all of Manhattan on the West Side from 42nd Street (roughly, Engine 65, which is located on 43rd Street between 5th/6th, is a part of Battalion 8) up to about 72nd Street, which includes Times Square, Rockefeller Center, Central Park South, parts of Hell's Kitchen, and Lincoln Center. Battalion 9 is also where Rescue 1 is officially located, although some people still believe that Rescue is located in Battalion 8. I have met numerous firefighters by name there, and will mention Firefighter Joe Maresca and Lieutenant Bob Jackson. On my last visit, I met additional firefighters by name, including Brian Siegel, Vinnie, Danny, and Bill. Also on my last visit, another "first" happened. For the first time, the firefighters invited me into the kitchen of the firehouse, a very hallowed spot of the firehouse. Vinnie was the one who invited me back, and I had some fun there, just sitting at the kitchen table, which had their company logo on it, talking to the guys. Two women also were there, and they had two prints of firemen raising the flag over the World Trade Center, and though I was a firefighter (I was wearing my Engine 292 shirt at the time, which had a lot of FDNY marking on it), and offered to let me sign it. When I told them I wasn't a firefighter (yet....), they didn't want me to sign it, even though I offered. On my last visit, I also saw Lieutenant Jackson again, and he was very pleased to see me.

Each time I have gone, I have had a great time, and 3 out of my last 5 visits, I've received a momento from the firefighters. In April of '98, the firefighters gave me a signed poster, in August of '01, my father and I bought a T-shirt, and in December of '01, I received a Sept. 11th memorial T-shirt. On my visit there in March of '02, I noticed that the riding lists for the night tour from Sept. 10th had been left intact, and that many memorials had been placed in the firehouse, which lost seventeen men on Sept. 11th. On my last visit, I saw that both companies were running spare rigs, which actually makes sense, given that both companies are very busy and that their rigs are constantly in need of repair. I also saw that new riding lists had been posted in the firehouse, and actually on Battalion 9's Ford Excursion, a small tribute had been placed on the rear window to the chief and his aide who had responded to the World Trade Center and been killed, namely Battalion Chief Edward Geraghty and Firefighter Alan Feinberg.

On a happier note, Engine 54 and Ladder 4 are among the few companies that have never been disbanded. During the 1950s and 1960s, Ladder 4 ran a tiller ladder. You're likely to spot 'em at any major fire in Manhattan, given that Ladder 4 has been the city's busiest ladder company for three years running ('99, 2000, '01). This firehouse also has a neon sign that says "Engine Company 54, Ladder Company 4, Battalion 9" like Engine 7/Ladder 1/Battalion 1. Although Ladder 4's rig was destroyed at the World Trade Center (which had just been obtained not more than a month before), they recovered a part of it from the World Trade Center site and easily obtained a new ladder truck, which was reassigned from the Bureau of Training. Engine 54's rig is due to be replaced as well, mainly because they have run the same rig for nine years, and it has taken a fair amount of street scars. Before Engine 54 ran their current 1993 Seagrave, they ran a 1983 Mack high-pressure Pumper, which was one of the last rigs in FDNY history to be painted entirely red. That rig actually was briefly seen in an episode of *Rescue 911*, when they chronicled an infamous fire on May 14, 1991 where members of Rescue 1 had to perform a rope rescue at a theater at 48th Street and 7th Avenue, and save men who were trapped on the 48th Street side and on the 7th Avenue side. Towards the end, when William Shatner narrates, "More than 100 firefighters fought the blaze for another hour before it was extinguished", for about 3 seconds, the front of their rig is seen, with a big red number "54" and with flashing lights. This firehouse also runs a fair amount of spare appartus, given that both companies are very busy, and that both probably get more than normal street scars and wear and tear. Heck, on my last visits, both companies were running spare rigs.

Their history dates back to the late 19th Century, and to their volunteer predecessors who predate them. Evidently the volunteer predesscor to Ladder 4 was on the same site (8th/48th). They are one of the best visits in the city, a short walk from everything. They still are a busy station, but often, you'll find someone around, and you'll have some fun! Go visit "The Pride of Midtown", and the company who "Never Missed a Performance", maybe you'll meet Joe Maresca, Lt. Jackson, Vinnie, Danny, Bill, or Brian Siegel, and you'll have a wonderful time!

Engine Company 23
215 West 58th Street

Author has particularly detailed knowledge thanks to kind tour by firefighters. Featured in the *AIA Guide to New York City*, Third Edition.

This firehouse comes very close to being a triple crown winner, the only reason they aren't is because I've never met any firefighters by name. My dad is the one who knows this firehouse. This little firehouse, on a quiet-side street right near the Hard Rock Cafe, is a beautiful piece of architecture that has been well-kept over the years, including a major renovation in 1998. During that time, Engine 23 was quartered with Engine 40/Ladder 35 on Amsterdam Avenue behind Lincoln Center. The firehouse was also the home to Ladder 4 when new quarters were being built for them in the early '70s. Engine 23's responsibility is Columbus Circle (where 8th Avenue meets Broadway and becomes Central Park West and meets Central Park South), which includes the Trump Towers, Central Park South, and a large portion of Midtown due south of Central Park, and Central Park itself. Their exterior look is somewhat deceiving, because on the inside, there is room for an entire second rig behind Engine 23. I think they ran a spare there for a while, but on my last visit, it was just Engine 23. To tell the truth, I honestly am not sure why they don't run a Brush Fire Unit (BFU) out of Engine 23's house in the event of a major conflagration in Central Park. Furthermore, there are BFU's in all the other boroughs (including a whopping 5 in Staten Island), and even though I suspect actual brush fires in Central Park are relatively low, the city should probably run a BFU just in case. Plus, if Engine 23 could run a spare out of here for a while and at one time Ladder 4, they can easily run a BFU. FDNY, give it some thought! They are also Engine 54/Ladder 4/Battalion 9's little friend. On my visit to the city in June of '02, I saw that they had acquired a beautiful brand new rig from where I was staying, because they got a run somewhere off Central Park West. Also on that same visit, their garage door had been repainted with an American Flag and their mascot, the Lion, on it and remembering the members of Engine 23 who were killed on September 11th. They call themselves the "Lion's Den", and actually they have a small statue of a lion next to the firehouse door. Go visit them, and maybe you'll be compelled to draw too!

Engine 5's quarters on 14th Street, near the Stuveysant Town housing complex. This firehouse was renovated between 1998 and 1999, but traces of the old FDNY still live on in it, specifically, in the font of the words "ENGINE COMPANY 5". This firehouse's door also is one of a rare breed, it actually has a lot of windows, as opposed to most other doors, that only contain two. (Joseph Schneiderman Photo)

Engine 14's quarters on 18th Street near Union Square. If one looks with careful detail, one will see a green decoration of some sort, possibly holly near the writing "14 ENGINE 14". This firehouse, ironically enough, is at 14 East 18th Street, and one can see the street address on the door (not the bay door) to the firehouse. (Joseph Schneiderman Photo)

Engine 8/Ladder 2/Battalion 8's quarters on 51st Street in Midtown. This firehouse, like Engine 4/Ladder 15/Decon Trailer's quarters in the Financial District, is also built into a high-rise building, and is responsible for a fair amount of high-rises in its response district. Battalion 8 even calls itself "The High-Rise Capital of the World" on its patches. (Joseph Schneiderman Photo)

Engine 54/Ladder 4/Battalion 9's quarters on 8th Avenue, at 48th Street near Times Square. Although there are two separate bays for the engine, truck, and battalion chief, there is no wall between the rigs on the inside of their quarters, unlike many other firehouses where a battalion or division is quartered. Ladder 4 once occupied this very site alone, with Battalion 9's quarters immeaditly behind them on 48th Street. (Joseph Schneiderman Photo)

Constructed from steel at the World Trade Center site, this small tribute to the brave men of Engine 54/Ladder 4/Battalion 9 now hangs over the kitchen in their quarters. This firehouse had the single greatest loss of any firehouse in the department, losing seventeen men at the World Trade Center. (Joseph Schneiderman Photo)

Engine 23's quarters on 58th Street in Midtown Manhattan. This firehouse, also called "The Lion's Den", also lost a fair amount of men on September 11th at the World Trade Center (8), and never had that painting on their door. If you look closely, you can see a small statue of a lion next to the firehouse bay door. (Joseph Schneiderman Photo)

So concludes Midtown. We're almost out of firehouses to visit in the city! But, we still have some in uptown, and we have an entire borough left! So hang on baby!

Engine Company 40, Ladder Company 35
131-133 Amsterdam Avenue, at West 66th Street

Author knows particular firefighter(s) here by name. Author has particularly detailed knowledge.

This is probably one of the smallest if not the smallest firehouse in the city! Although it is built into a high-rise building (like Engine 4/Ladder 15 and Engine 8/Ladder 2/Battalion 8), it takes up minimal space on the southeast corner of Amsterdam and 66th. When I visited, there was relatively minimal space between the rigs, and the housewatch was particularly small, and there was a very small lounge adjoining the appartus bay. Furthermore, there is very little space behind the rigs and behind them, but the firehouse is a nice one, considering it is so small. The firehouse also actually says on the facade above the bays "Fire Department of the City of New York", but in a very small font.

Engine 40 and Ladder 35 are located in the 9th Battalion, along with Engine 54/Ladder 4 and Engine 23. Ladder 35 is a tower ladder, but not a 95 footer (all of you who are getting sick of my jabbering about 95 footers probably must have had a breath of relief), a typical 75 footer. Engine 40 is a normal engine company, not a high-pressure company or a 2000 gallon per minute pumper, but it is one of a few engine companies that I have seen with the numbers on its grill almost like hood ornaments. Ladder 35 currently runs a Seagrave, but their old Mack CF tower ladder can also be seen in the same episode of *Rescue 911* where we saw Engine 54's rig. This firehouse's responsibility is Lincoln Center and the surrounding neighborhood, which includes Lincoln Square (where Columbus Avenue meets Broadway) and the housing complex named after it, Central Park, the downtown campus of Fordham University, the John Jay College of Criminal Justice, and parts of the prestigious Upper West Side. This firehouse would probably respond to major runs with Engine

23 at Columbus Circle, and could easily get called to Sherman Square (where Amsterdam Avenue meets Broadway).

Engine 40 and Ladder 35 was probably one of the most publicized firehouses in the wake of the September 11th attack on the World Trade Center, and one reason for that publicity is probably because the only member of the 9th Battalion not missing there was from that house, a Firefighter by the name of Kevin Shea. All the rest of the members from the 9th Battalion who responded, except for him, were missing. On my visit, the mood of the firefighters seemed exceptional, given that they had lost their captain, Captain Frank Callahan, who evidently was a very famous man, and ten more of their brothers in battle had been killed. On this same note, the *New York Times Magazine* did an article on Kevin Shea after September 11th, mainly on the effect that losing his brothers in battle had on him, and his experience of amnesia after the World Trade Center collapse. There was a photo in that article of him being found alive in some debris.

On a better note, Engine 40 and Ladder 35 have a unique motto, "The Cavemen", which makes close to no sense given their location. It is possible that "Cavemen" has something to do with Central Park. It could also be because their firehouse is so small, that it is built like a cave. I personally am amazed that Fred Astaire or something else Lincoln Center related isn't their mascot or motto. On my visit, I also saw that the typical FDNY signage that is on the facade above the firehouse doors was on the inside of their firehouse. Go visit these "Cavemen", and you'll find that they are not living in the prehistoric era, instead, in the era of firefighting in New York City, protecting Lincoln Center!

Engine Company 22, Ladder Company 13, Battalion 10
159 East 85th Street, between Lexington and 3rd Avenue

This is the only firehouse my dad photographed before I had seen it. It is a near twin to Engine 3/Ladder 12/Battalion 7. On my last visit some German firefighters were visiting. All I know is that Ladder 13 is a tower ladder, and that they've always been in that area, mainly because their FQ is on 86th. This firehouse's primary responsibility is places like the

Metropolitan Museum of Art and the prestigious Upper East Side, and a neighborhood known as Yorkville, which actually is included on this company's patch. Their motto also is in German, namely "Mehr Damen Dann Flamen". Their patch is also the only patch I know of to feature a woman on it (a picture of a woman serving beers or some other drinks, like that brand of beer with such a picture). This firehouse was also recently featured in the *New York Times* because the Metropolitan Museum of Art had decided to help them preserve their riding lists from September 10th/11th. After all, the Metropolitan Museum of Art is right down the street from them!

There actually is a rather touching story involving this firehouse and a certain Yankee pitcher. In the wake of the September 11th attack at the World Trade Center, Yankee ace Roger Clemens and his teammates wanted to visit a firehouse to try to lift their spirits. The firehouse which Clemens found was this one (one wonders why he found this one and not Yankee Stadium's protection on Ogden Avenue or Squad 41 on 150th), and Clemens wears on his jersey, ironically enough, #22. So, when he visited this house, he gave them a signed jersey which read "To the men of Engine Co. 22, from one 22 to another".

Buffs, please go visit and find me some more info!

Engine Company 53, Ladder Company 43
1836 3rd Avenue at 102nd Street

Featured in the *AIA Guide to New York City*, Third Edition. Author requests readers to send in more information.

"El Barrio's Bravest", they protect the lower parts of Harlem, and have the 23rd Precinct as their left-hand neighbor. They are also the FQ of the now disbanded Division 4. They also are the northernmost house in the 10th Battalion. Engine 53's FQ was also featured in the *AIA Guide* (see also Engine 54/Ladder 4/Battalion 9). This firehouse also runs a R.A.C. (Rehabiliation and Comfort) unit, namely R.A.C. 1, and they run the only R.A.C. on Manhattan's mainland. R.A.C. 4 is quartered at Special Operations Command's (abbreviated S.O.C.) headquarters on Roosevelt

Island, and although technically Roosevelt Island is a part of Manhattan, R.A.C. 4 would have somewhat of a difficult time responding to fires in Manhattan. Buffs, go visit 'em and give me info!

Engine Company 58, Ladder Company 26
1367 5th Avenue

The "Fire Factory", they protect the northern tip of Central Park, and also some of Central Harlem. They are also one of the few if not the only firehouse actually located on 5th Avenue. This firehouse also is part of the 12th Battalion (which we'll see shortly...). A note to all the parents out there: Firefighters from this house were recently seen on Sesame Street. Engine 58 was also a participant or victim (you be the judge) of the FDNY's experiment with chartreuse. Buffs, I need info, so go visit.

And now, our final firehouse in Manhattan:

Engine Company 35, Ladder Company 14, 12th Battalion
2282 3rd Avenue., between 124th and 125th Street at the base of the Triborough Bridge

This firehouse is a modern and mundane firehouse, akin to Engine 71/Ladder 55/Division 6. They provide reliable fire protection and Engine 35 carries the honor of being the oldest company in Harlem, dating back to 1807. Ladder 14 also has called themselves "Tower Power", and more recently "Super-Tower". Battalion 12's slogan is much like Battalion 6's, except different, namely, "Heaven in Harlem", and they have similar patches. At one time Ladder 14 ran an American LaFrance tower ladder unlike the other tower ladders in the city, which ran Mack CF/Aerial-scopes. Furthermore, as I keep jabbering on about, they run the only 95 foot tower ladder in Division 3! Ladder 14 also evidently gets special-called to certain fires in the Bronx, even though Battalion 12 is still in Division 3 and not Division 6 or 7, which are responsible for the Bronx and Upper Manhattan. Battalion 12 also has been consistently quartered with Ladder 14. Ladder 14 also was briefly seen in the documentary

"Firemen in the Bronx", which aired on PBS, and they were seen at a factory fire, along with a couple of other tower ladders, like Ladder 17 from the Bronx, which is my basis for saying that they get special called to the Bronx. Unfortunately, like the rest of them in Uptown, I need info! So, buffs, please give me some info on these guys!

Engine 40/Ladder 35's quarters on Amsterdam Avenue near Lincoln Center. This firehouse is also built into a high-rise building, namely, 166 W. 66th Street. This firehouse, despite being into a high-rise, is probably one of the smallest in the city, as the interior is not particularly large. (Joseph Schneiderman Photo)

The wall above housewatch in Engine 40/Ladder 35's quarters. Typically,company citations and firehouse nostalgia are placed on the wall above the housewatch, as is the case here. (Joseph Schneiderman Photo)

Now, some *POSSIBLE TRIPS* for the buffs to consider:

Starting in Lower Manhattan, again. Engine 4/Ladder 15/Decon Trailer, Engine Company 6, Ladder Company 20, the Fire Store, Engine 33/Ladder 9, Engine 55, and the FQ of Engine 31. You can catch the 5 train to Brooklyn Bridge/City Hall station, visit Engine 6, then catch the 6 (Lexington Avenue. Local) train to Spring Street and it is a 1 minute walk to Ladder 20 and the Fire Store. There is also a nice little deli which sells new age sort of food and old good stuff on the northwest corner of Spring and Lafayette, right above the Spring Street subway station. It is a short walk from there to FQ of Engine 31 or Engine 55. In fact, you can walk down Spring Street from Ladder 20 and the Fire Store to the fire museum. It's a little bit of a walk, but it's a good walk just the same. In that vicinity, the A, C, or E trains can take you to Canal Street, and from there it is a short walk to Ladder 8. Another nice thing to do if you're visiting Engine 4/Ladder 15/Decon Trailer is visit Battery Park or take the Staten Island Ferry. Additionally, at 100 Old Slip, which is a stone's throw from Engine 4/Ladder 15/Decon Trailer is the Police Museum, which is located in the former 1st Precinct (now on Ericson Place in TriBeCa), considered to be the first modern police station in New York City. A fairly direct route to Engine 4/Ladder 15/Decon Trailer is to take the M15 bus (First Avenue and Second Avenue Bus) down to Old Slip or Goveurneur Lane (at that point it runs along Water Street), and walk out Old Slip or Goveurneur Lane. Additionally, City Hall is a stone's throw from Engine 6 or Engine 7/Ladder 1/Battalion 1, as is the Brooklyn Bridge from Engine 6.

In a super downtown buffing trip, one can visit all the firehouses in the 1st Battalion through a lot of walking or a lot of subways! Starting at the bottom, take the 1 or 2 train to Wall Street. Walk out Wall Street to South Street (a nice short, and lively walk), and south past Gouverneur Lane, and you'll find Engine 4/Ladder 15. When the Ten House is reopened, it is not particularly much of a walk to that house from Engine 4/Ladder 15. Then walk back to Wall Street, catch the 1 or 2 train northbound to the subway hub at Fulton Street/Broadway-Nassau, and from there you can catch an A,C, J, M,Z, 4 or 5 train. The A or C can take you to Chambers Street, and from there it is a short walk to Engine 7/Ladder 1/Battalion 1, and then you can walk across City Hall Park to Engine 6 on Beekman Street. Alternatively, you can catch a 4 or 5 train to Brooklyn Bridge-City Hall, and then walk south along Park Row to Beekman Street to Engine 6, then walk across City Hall Park to Engine 7/Ladder 1/Battalion 1.

The walk to visit all the houses in Battalion 1 would probably work something like this (excluding The Ten House): Starting at the corner of State Street and South Street (one of the southernmost points in Manhattan), walk up South Street to Engine 4/Ladder 15's quarters, walk out Wall Street to Broadway, walk up Broadway to Fulton Street, walk north on Park Row to Beekman Street, walk east on Beekman Street to Engine 6, then walk back out Beekman to Park Row, and cut across City Hall Park back to Broadway, and walk up Broadway to Duane Street, and walk west on Duane Street to Engine 7/Ladder 1/Battalion 1's quarters. The walk would not significantly change with the inclusion of the Ten House, just walk up Broadway to Liberty Street as opposed to Fulton Street, and walk west on Liberty Street to the Ten House. From there, you have your choice of walking to Engine 7/Ladder 1/Battalion 1 (a short walk north on Church Street, then east on Duane Street), or walking back out to Broadway and up to Park Row to visit Engine 6's house.

To get to Engine 33/Ladder 9 from the Fire Store, catch a cab north on Lafayette or take the 6 train to Bleecker Street or Astor Place (buffs, you'll have to check me on that). In Midtown, the 1 or 2 train can get you to Engine 3/Ladder 12/Battalion 7 at 18th Street, and then from Penn Station/34th Street, it is a short walk to Engine 1/Ladder 24. There is also the 14th Street Crosstown Bus which can help you get from Union Square to Chelsea or just around that part of Manhattan, given the 14th Street is a big crosstown throughfare.

On the note of Union Square and that region, one can potentially visit all the firehouses in Battalion 6 as a Downtown/Midtown trip. The #6 train can take you to Bleecker Street or Astor Place (your choice) which is a stone's throw from Engine 33/Ladder 9 (which I just mentioned). Then catch the #6 train to Union Square-14th Street, visit Ladder 3/Battalion 6 and Engine 14 by walking between them, then catch the "L" train (14th Street-Canarsie Local) to 1st Avenue, and visit Engine 5.

The firehouses in Union Square are all within walking distance of each other. The C or the E train (8th Avenue Local) can get you to 50th Street, and it's a short walk south on 8th Avenue to Engine 54/Ladder 4/ Battalion 9. Rescue 1 lies north and west from 42nd Street Station off the A (8th Avenue Express), C, or E, and Engine 23 is a nice and easy walk north on 8th and east on 58th from Engine 54/Ladder 4/Battalion 9. In fact, one can take on subway line between Engine 54/Ladder 4/Battalion 9 and Engine 8/Ladder 2/Battalion 8, the E train. I've never done it, but it can be done! The reason one can go crosstown like that is because the E train becomes the Queens Boulevard line in Queens, and it has to get to Queens somehow, right? Well, the E train will take you to 50th Street as aforementioned, and then if you board the E again, it will turn east, and it can take you to Lexington Avenue/53rd Street station, which connects to 51st Street station of the 6 train, which is a 1 minute walk from Engine 8/Ladder 2/Battalion 8.

Another fun thing to do at Engine 54/Ladder 4/Battalion 9, if you have a huge appetite for meat, is to go the Churrascaria Plataforma Restaurant on 49th Street west of 8th Avenue. They serve entire slabs of meat, and you don't order it, the waiters come around and bring it to you! It's the perfect post-buffing meal. Make sure you save room for dessert, the desserts are incredible.

In the vicinity of Rescue 1, the Circle Line is a fun trip, and the *U.S.S. Intrepid* is also a fun look at aviation and the military.

Speaking of Battalion 9, one can visit all the companies in it in a day, just like Battalion 1 or Battalion 6, in a combined Midtown-Uptown trip. Rescue 1 is where we start, which is a bit of a walk from 42nd Street/ Port Authority Bus Terminal off the A, C, or E train, but one can take the 42nd Street Crosstown Bus to 11th Avenue, and from there, it's a short walk. Then catch the same bus back to 42nd Street subway station or catch an 8th Avenue bus. If you choose to take the subway, you'll want a C or E train to 50th Street, and from there, just walk down 8th Avenue to Engine 54/Ladder 4/Battalion 9. From there, you can walk, take an 8th Avenue bus, or take the C train to Engine 23. The walk is up 8th Avenue and east across 58th Street over to Engine 23, the 8th Avenue bus can also take you to 58th Street, and C train takes you to Columbus Circle-59th Street, and from there it's also a short walk. After Engine 23, catch the 1 or 2 train north to Lincoln Square-66th Street, and walk west on 66th out to Amsterdam, and Engine 40/Ladder 35 is in plain sight. You can also probably walk to all those firehouses, but be prepared for a walk equivalent to the Battalion 1 walk! I actually visited 3 out of the 4 of those firehouses on my last visit to New York City! But the 3 non-S.O.C. firehouses are sufficient enough to visit Battalion 9!

Uptown, there are a few trips I can recommend, but only one trip I have formulated, but it's a dandy. Engine 22/Ladder 13/Battalion 10 is but a block south on 3rd Avenue from Papaya King. All I'm gonna say is go to Papaya King for a snack right before going to Engine 22/Ladder 13/Battalion 10, or right afterward. Additionally, if for some reason you need to get to Pelham Bay Park from that part of Manhattan, the BxM 7A express bus runs there, and it stops in Pelham Bay Park. In the vicinity of Engine 40/Ladder 35, there is a nice Barnes and Noble at Lincoln Square, and other shopping there too. The 1 or 2 train can take you there. If you choose to, you can also visit Engine 22/Ladder 13/Battalion 10, Engine 53/Ladder 43 and Engine 35/Ladder 14/Battalion 12 in a single trip too. The #6 train (damn, we do a lot with the 6 train!) takes you to 86th Street, then circle the block to get to Engine 22/Ladder 13/Battalion 10, then reboard and take it to 103rd Street, and you can walk to 3rd Avenue relatively quickly to get to Engine 53/Ladder 43, and then the 6 can take you to 125th Street, and from there it is also a short walk to Engine 35/Ladder 14/Battalion 12. But security is an issue in those areas, so keep your witts about you and be quick. So concludes Manhattan. One more borough. So sad. Oh well.

7

STATEN ISLAND

A little borough, one of the few boroughs that still has grassland, it also has the least protection, but that is understandable, as only 370,000 people live there. Many of them are firefighters who work in other boroughs. Eighteen firehouses protect the borough, many of them solo engine companies, but Staten Island also has a solo ladder company. Staten Island also the home of the fireboat *Firefighter*, more commonly known as Marine Company 9. Quartered on Front Street, the *Firefighter* has been in service since 1936! So, let's begin our journey in Staten Island, and the four firehouses I know.

Engine Company 154, BFU (Brush Fire Unit) 4
3730 Victory Boulevard

Author has particularly detailed knowledge. Featured in the *AIA Guide to New York City*, Third Edition.

A modern firehouse, which at one time probably housed a ladder company, because their facade is similar to Engine 72's, namely "ENGINE 154 LADDER". Currently, they protect some of the wetlands and I believe they protect the now closed Fresh Kills Landfill and the neighborhood known as Travis, once known as "Lineolumville" because of all the Linoleum plants located there.

This firehouse also seems to be one farthest west in Staten Island, given that the Goethals Bridge is not particularly far away. Their motto is "Splendor in the Grass", which makes sense, given that they are located in a particularly grassy area, and that they run a BFU. The multicolored shirt that Eagle Emblems produced for them has both their rigs against the grassy background of their neighborhood and with the Con Edison oil containers on fire Engine 154 has also been disbanded twice, in fact, it was disbanded twice in the same year. In 1975, there was a big budget crunch in the department. Thirty-two companies, mostly engine companies were disbanded, but some were reorganized. One day that will probably stick in the minds of all the firefighters who worked then is July 2, 1975. On that day, many companies were disbanded only to be reorganized two days later on July 4th. Engine 154 was one of those. Finally, in November of that year, they were disbanded again, seemingly for good. But in 1981 they were reorganized, and have stayed in their Victory Boulevard firehouse ever since. It's very weird and quirky. On the note of Engine 154's company across the floor (the term for the ladder companies or any other companies quartered at a firehouse, like if a firefighter is stationed at Engine 258, but works a shift or becomes a member of Ladder 115, he is said to be moving across the floor), BFU 4, they run a unique rig, a surplus Air Force Crash Rescue Truck, converted to Brush Firefighting. Evidently the city purchased at least two such apparatus, as on a visit to an FDNY apparatus site, I saw that same rig as a special Haz-Mat rig. A Foam Unit, Foam 154 is also quartered here. They also have a volunteer, yes volunteer neighbor, a few blocks west that is worth a mention, **Oceanic Hook and Ladder 1**. Although Oceanic is relatively obscure, both are worth a visit, especially at the same time.

Engine Company 160, Rescue Company 5, Division 8, Tactical Support Unit 2
1850 Clove Road

Author has particularly detailed knowledge thanks to kind tour by firefighters.

This firehouse sounds like it could be pretty large, but in truth, it isn't that big. They also have a large parking lot in front for all kinds of support units. Rescue 5 is known as "Blue Thunder", and they are responsible for a good deal of water rescues on Staten Island, and that's why Tac (or TSU, either one is appropriate FDNY colloquial) 2 is with them, because the Tac units provide water support. The Tac units actually don't just handle water rescues, but other sorts of rescue scenarios that Rescue Companies might handle also, because the Rescue trucks can only carry so much equipment. For anyone who's wondering, Tac 1 is on Roosevelt Island at S.O.C. (Special Operations Command) Headquarters, and there are only two TSU's in the city.

Rescue 5 actually was disbanded for a while, between circa 1964 and 1984, but they were reorganized and received a spiffy new Mack "R" rig, which was standard for the rescue companies to be running at that time. Rescue 5 also was featured in the documentary "Brothers in Battle", made by the late Captain Brian Hickey of Rescue Company 4. Sadly, Capt. Hickey was one of the 343 members killed on September 11th (see also Queens Engine 292/Rescue 4). Rescue 5's fame in that documentary was a water rescue they performed with Engine 152 (another Staten Island company), The U.S. Coast Guard, and some aid from an NYPD helicopter on one of the bases of the Verrazano Bridge. Rescue 5 also runs a Haz-Mat support van. All of the squad companies run one as a second piece for major fires, but because there is not currently a squad on Staten Island (yet...), Rescue 5 runs Staten Island's. Rescue 5 also was prominently featured in John Calderone's The History of Fire Engines. Division 8 also is a unique division, in that they have three battalions in Staten Island and three in southwestern Brooklyn. Division 8 was also (get a load of this!!!) disbanded in 1975 (on the same day that many other companies were disbanded, no not July 2nd, November 22nd), and didn't return to service until 1990, at about the same time that Engine 41 returned! They are a great visit!

Engine Company 166, Ladder Company 86
1400 Richmond Avenue

Author has particularly detailed knowledge thanks to kind tours by firefighters. Author knows particular firefighter(s) here by name.

This firehouse, although a modern one in terms of architecture, is home to the second largest 2 digit ladder company in the city, and is relatively close to the Staten Island Mall. They are also right off the Staten Island Expressway, and across from the Staten Island Hotel. This firehouse also has "R.A.F." as their motto. I still haven't quite figured out what they mean, but I can assume that it might have something to do with Richmond Avenue. Go visit these central Staten Island firefighters!
Our last firehouse. Sniff. At least they're a doozy.

Ladder Company 79, Battalion 22
1189 Castleton Avenue.

Featured in the *AIA Guide to New York City,* Third Edition. Author has particularly detailed knowledge thanks to kind tours by firefighters. Author requests readers to send in more information.

These guys win a triple crown, but they win a different one. They are one of the more famous companies in the city, probably the most famous one from Staten Island. They protect the North Shore of Staten Island, as their company motto tells us, "North Shore Trucking Company"; and they are a tower ladder. At one time they were Ladder 104, and before that, they were Medora Ladder 3, a volunteer company. Ladder 104 now is a tiller ladder company in Brooklyn, in Williamsburg, I believe. Also, this firehouse was mistakenly listed as Engine 79 in the *AIA Guide to New York City.* Engine 79 is quartered in the Bronx, with Ladder 37 and Battalion 27, in the northwestern area of the borough, near Woodlawn. Ladder 79's firehouse also has been immortalized by the company Code 3 Collectibles, given that they made a 1/64 scale model of it for sale for a whopping $125.00 (expensive!). Battalion 22 is also responsible for one-third of Staten Island's fire protection, including the port, and Engine 154/ BFU 4, and Engine 166/Ladder 86 are a part of Battalion 22. They are another great visit!

POSSIBLE TRIPS:

Engine 154/BFU 4, Engine 166/Ladder 86 and the Staten Island Mall; Ladder 79 and the Snug Harbor area. It is ideal to have a car on Staten Island, given that there is only one rapid transit line, and it runs along the east edge of the borough. There is also a nifty deli near the Staten Island Mall that has an old BMT subway car inside of it, where patrons can eat! On most of my visits to Staten Island with my dad, we have done that at that deli! That alone is a highlight of any trip to Staten Island! Buffs, please give me some help! Go figure out some trips, my friends!

Engine 154/BFU 4's quarters on Victory Boulevard in Staten Island. This picture reveals a fair amount about the firehouse just by looking at it. In the lower right corner, it is plain to see that the firehouse was constructed in 1971, and like Engine 72's quarters in the Bronx, this firehouse evidently housed or was meant to house a ladder company at one time. Now BFU 4 gets the ladder company's part of the floor. A closer look reveals flowers and a bulletin board, and the seal of the City of New York. (Henry Schneiderman Photo)

Oceanic Hook and Ladder 1's quarters further west on Victory Boulevard. Note how small the firehouse is in comparison to their paid
brothers in battle further east on Victory, and how they have an additional bay that was added to the original firehouse. Note also how the
font saying "Oceanic H&L CO. NO. 1" is reminiscent of those old
"WANTED" signs from the old west. If you look closely, you can also
see in the pavement beneath the firehouse a maltese cross saying
"Oceanic 1", and their date of organization, 1881. (Henry Schneiderman Photo)

8

THE BOROUGH PICKS

I bet that you thought we were all done after we visited Ladder 79/ Battalion 22. We ain't!!!! And yes, you still have to keep listening to my jabbering on and on about 95 foot tower ladders, high pressure pumpers, 2000 gallon per minute pumpers, BFU's, and everything else that I've been jabbering on and on and on and on about since the introduction.

Well, this chapter is all about my picks for city-wide buffing. In other words, the best firehouses to buff at in each borough will be lined up here. Now before we begin, I want to say this list only got into the book because I thought the buffs would like to know which firehouses I recommend as the best visits in each borough. Now to all the firefighters out there from companies who don't make this list, don't feel bad. It only means that I will probably have to stop by your firehouse and see the rigs and stuff, and maybe next time you will make it onto the "Borough Picks" list. Furthermore, I salute you all! You, the brothers in battle, who rush in when others rush out, are a large inspiration of this book! Your firehouses symbolize what you are, and don't think that I haven't not enjoyed a single firehouse in this book, because each one of you guys has been fun, whether I just passed you on the bus or in the car or got to go into the housewatch! To all the brothers, thank you all! And also, I love everyone of these firehouses equally. The ones that don't have a lot written about them is just because I don't know much about you! Oh well. To the ones that I have to visit again and get more info, I'll see you soon. To the ones with lots of info, you guys have found me and I have found you well. Thanks to all of you, the brothers.

Now, on with the Borough Picks. All of these firehouses have been selected carefully based on my experiences at them. Now in Manhattan, because I split it up into Uptown, Downtown and Midtown, I will pick a firehouse from each section, but not have a single one for the borough. Again, we will begin in Queens and end in Staten Island. Furthermore, each firehouse will have a reason as to why it is the borough pick. Well enough hooplah and procrastination, let's get started!

THE BOROUGH PICKS

Queens: Queens is a bit of a tough one, given that I've only been to 5 houses total there, so I don't have much choice. So, this one is a rather tentative award, and it could change once I have visited more firehouses there, but I give the Borough Pick in Queens to Engine 292/Rescue 4 on Queens Boulevard. The men there were so nice to me, and also the firehouse is a dynamic site, especially with urban decay and the effects of urbanization right near by. Rescue companies are also always a good visit, and given that I met the senior man on Rescue 4, Mike Milner, and him and Firefighters Naviasky and Mahoney and I talked for so long, and just had a lot of fun, and Lieutenant Roche was pleased to meet me. Rescue 4, as a company anyway, also seems very jovial given that they lost so many men at the World Trade Center. Little children also will probably like seeing Popeye as a fireman and the idea of the "Winfield Cougars" might appeal to them. Additionally, there is a lot of history bottled up in that firehouse. Thus, for all those reasons, Engine 292/Rescue 4 earns my award for the Borough Pick for Queens.

Brooklyn: This one actually is easy and hard at the same time, given that recently I've had some very good times at some houses all over the borough, but mainly have been to houses in Downtown Brooklyn or Brooklyn Heights. Ah, what the hell. I'll get on with it. Engine 207/Ladder 110/

Satellite 6/FCU 1 and 2/Battalion 31/Division 11 wins the Brooklyn Borough Pick award. It wins for many of the same reasons that Engine 292/ Rescue 4 won for Queens. Little children will be amazed at the diversity of rigs there, and they probably also will like the fact that the companies are known as the "Tillary Street Tigers". Little children (and adults for that matter) can also relate to the idea of the "Island of Misfit Toys", which is what they call themselves too, because they run such a diversity of rigs. History buffs (Firefighting or otherwise) will like the history at that house, and the Downtown Brooklyn neighborhood is so nice, especially with the Fulton Mall and Metrotech Center. Also, the firefighters there offered to let me go on a run with them, which gives the house a very dear place in my heart. The firehouse's neighborhood is also relatively safe (which it hadn't been for a while), and there is a police precinct right behind them on Gold Street if any trouble does happen. That and also, my dad loves this house, probably almost as much as I do, and wants to accompany me back there to meet my friends. Anyway, Engine 207/Ladder 110/Satellite 6/FCU 1 and 2/Battalion 31/Division 11 wins my pick for Brooklyn! Congratulations to the "Tillary Street Tigers" and "The Island of Misfit Toys", you aren't as misfit after all!

'Da Bronx: Hoo boy. This is probably the toughest choice of them all. After all, these firehouse are extremes, so to speak, meaning I've been inside them and had the time of my life, or just passed by for the briefest of moments. Well, this is even tougher than I thought, especially because my beloved mother is from the Bronx. Well, I think I'll have to declare a four way tie between the following houses: namely Engine 38/Ladder 51, Engine 70/Ladder 53, Engine 72/Satellite 2, and Engine 89/Ladder 50. Engine 38/Ladder 51 is fairly obvious, given that they sent me up in the tower ladder and their house is in a nice neighborhood, Engine 70/Ladder 53 because they are on City Island and there's food and great views and a nice playground for little kids at the south tip of the island, Engine 72 and Satellite 2 because they run the satellite for the Bronx, also because they win a triple crown and still run a Mack, and are first due on anything that happens on the Throgs Neck Bridge or Bronx-Whitestone Bridge, and Engine 89/Ladder 50 because they were and still are first due on anything that happens at Pelham Bay Park and my grandma's house. That and also Ladder 50 is a 95 foot tower ladder (just kidding!).

Manhattan: Like I said, we have three sections to pick bests from. So let's going! As a reminder, Lower Manhattan is defined as Battery Park and Bowling Green up to 14th Street, Midtown is 14th Street to 59th Street, and Uptown is 59th Street onwards.

Lower Manhattan: Oh boy. This is just as tough as the picks for the Bronx. Then again, it actually might be easy. Again I'm going to award a four way tie, this time to Engine 4/Ladder 15/Decon Trailer, Engine 7/Ladder 1/Battalion 1, Ladder 20/Medical Division/Division 1, and Engine 33/Ladder 9. The reasons for each one are very clear. Engine 4/Ladder 15/Decon Trailer is an easy trip to combine with Wall Street, the Police Museum, Battery Park, the South Street Seaport, and the rest of extreme lower Manhattan! Buffs of all types will also probably enjoy Ladder 10's rig while they are still quartered there, and hard-core buffs will probably enjoy the Decon Trailer. Engine 4 and Ladder 15 also have a unique layout in their appartus bay, and Engine 4 runs (they were running it at my last visit) a nifty Mack Pumper, and Ladder 15 is a tower ladder too. Engine 7/Ladder 1/Battalion 1 is a very historic firehouse and very close to City Hall, and history buffs will enjoy seeing the layout of the firehouse. That and also this firehouse has kind of become a part of common American vocabulary and knowledge after the events of September 11th and the film "9-11". The firehouse is also a good choice for architectural buffs. Ladder 20/Medical Division/Division 1 is a borough pick because little children will definitely like seeing the tiller ladder, and the men of Ladder 20 are some of the nicest firefighters in the department. Additionally, Ladder 20 is in a very central location in SoHo, where it is not hard to get to Chinatown, Little Italy, Greenwich Village, the East Village, the Lower East Side or the Financial District. Also, Ladder 20's neighbors, the Fire Store, is always fun. Engine 33 and Ladder 9 made the borough picks for one very good reason: It is probably my dad's favorite firehouse in the city aside from Engine 23 in Midtown. Engine 33/Ladder 9 also made the list because they simply are, outstanding as a piece of architecture. Furthermore, their location, even though they are near the particularly cruddy Bowery, is particularly prestigious, and the East Village has other nice architecture. So Dad, you can be proud that reading to your kid those many times about Engine 33 in the *AIA Guide* worked, because it made his borough picks list!

Midtown Manhattan: This actually is probably the toughest one of them all. Given that I know so much about so many of them, and also that friends of mine have friends at Ladder 2, this is a big toughie too! Oh well. Well given that I've awarded some ties, I'll award one again. This time my tie goes between Engine 8/Ladder 2/Battalion 8, Engine 23, and Engine 54/Ladder 4/Battalion 9. Engine 8/Ladder 2/Battalion 8 is a nifty firehouse in and of itself, given that it is built into a high-rise building, and there are many sites in the neighborhood. Little children also can relate to Snoopy (Ladder 2's mascot, as we discussed), and the rigs at that house are beauties. Engine 23 also made my list partially because of my dad. I have come to love that house just as he did, and even though I've only been inside once, I can see what he saw in it. That and also, Engine 23 has a nifty new rig. That and also, my mom likes lions. So, "Lion's Den" gets my other pick for Midtown. Engine 54/Ladder 4/Battalion 9 need not be explained, just go back to its listing in Midtown, and you'll see why it is borough pick. On another note, those firehouses are all within one or two subways of one another.

Uptown Manhattan: This one is kind of tough too, mainly because I haven't been to that many houses in Uptown. Oh well, I guess I'll throw out another tie, this time between Engine 40/Ladder 35 and Engine 22/Ladder 13/Battalion 10. Both are in majestic neighborhoods, with Central Park near Engine 40/Ladder 35 and the Metropolitan Museum of Art near Engine 22/Ladder 13/Battalion 10. Also Papaya King is in Engine 22/Ladder 13/Battalion 10's area.

Staten Island: Again, this one is a very tough call, especially because I've only been to four houses total. I think rather than award a borough pick to one firehouse, I will give them to all four firehouses (Engine 154/BFU 4, Engine 160/Rescue 5/Division 8/TSU 2, Engine 166/Ladder 86, and

Ladder 79/Battalion 22), given that I really have not been to enough fire-houses on Staten Island to warrant giving a borough pick. Engine 154/BFU 4 is a good bet because they run that unique Air Force Crash Rescue Truck, and Oceanic 1 is a short drive away from them. Engine 160/Rescue 5 is a good visit mainly because Rescue companies as a rule are good visits, and the firehouse is architecturally beautiful. Old TV buffs also will enjoy seeing Engine 160's motto, namely, "The Hillbillies". Engine 166/Ladder 86 is a good visit because they are right off the SIE (Staten Island Expressway), and very close to the Staten Island Mall and Staten Island Hotel. The firehouse also runs a tower ladder, and Engine 166's current rig is one of the more famous ones in FDNY history, mainly because it was on the cover of *Fire Apparatus Journal* AND *The History of Fire Engines*. The guys there are also all very nice. Finally, Ladder 79/Battalion 22 is probably the most famous company in Staten Island aside from Rescue 5, and buffs of all ages will enjoy that house, and finally be able to visit this highly publicized house. So again, all four houses here win the borough pick. Once I visit more houses, I probably will narrow it down to two. Then again, maybe not.

EPILOGUE

Well, we've been to 55 firehouses in the majestic City of New York. One hundred and seven companies total (phew!), 50 engine companies, 35 ladder companies, 3 rescue companies, fifteen battalions, and four divisions at least, not bad! But I think this epilogue is not an end, but a beginning. These 55 firehouses are merely a base for all you buffs to build on. These are only 55 suggestions, not definites. It is still in your hands as the buff to go to firehouses and find new ones, and tell me about them. For new buffs, this end is your beginning, to go out and explore firehouses. For established buffs, you have 55 chances to increase your knowledge or visit old favorites. The firehouses not mentioned in here are what Hamlet or Capt. Kirk would call "The Undiscovered Country", as they are out there, waiting for buffs to explore them. I hope all you buffs regard the end of our journey to 55 firehouses as not the end, but the beginning. Boy, I am contradicting myself royally, ain't I? Oh well. My last words are: Thank you for reading, God bless you, and never stop buffing!

FOR FURTHER INFORMATION:

A. Books

1. Sheila Buff. *Fire Engines in North America.* Secaucus, NJ: Wellfleet Press; 1991.

2. John A Calderone. *The History of Fire Engines.* New York: Barnes & Noble; 1997.

3. Ellen Freudenheim. *Brooklyn! A Soup to Nuts Guide to Sights, Neighborhoods, and Restaurants.* New York: Street Martins Griffin; 1999.

4. Robert Hall. *Fire Trucks in Action.* Osceloa, WI: Motorbooks International;1994.

5. Kenneth T Jackson, editor. *The Encyclopedia of New York City.* New Haven: Yale University Press; 1995.

6. Battalion Chief (Retired) Edwin F Schneider, 42nd Battalion, F.D.N.Y.. *A Fire Chief Remembers: Tales of the FDNY.* New Albany, IN: Fire Buff House Publishers; 1992.

7. Dennis Smith. *Report from Engine Company 82.* New York: Warner Books; 1972, 1999.

8. Dennis Smith. *Report from Ground Zero.* New York: The Penguin Group; 2002.

9. Elliot Willensky and Norval White. *AIA Guide to New York City.* Third ed. San Diego and New York: Harcourt Brace Jovanovich, Publishers; 1988.

B. Web Sites

1. **NYC.gov/html/fdny/html/home2.html**

   The F.D.N.Y.'s official website, containing a history of Manhattan's companies and a slideshow of the history of EMS in New York City.

2. **NYFD.com**

   Run by former Brooklyn firefighter Donald Van Holt of Ladder 103, Ladder 108, and Engine 216, it contains everything and anything about the fire department, including a comprehensive history compiled by Staten Island Fire Dispatcher Mike Boucher, links to other sites, you name it!

3. **NYFirestore.com**

   The official web site of the Fire Store, one can buy T-shirts from Manhattan, Brooklyn, you name it! They also sell hats, and one time they sold F.D.N.Y. related things for the kitchen.

4. **FDNYphotography.com**

   Run by professional photographer Robert Mitts, it contains many photos from major fires and historic fires, including the U.N. fire of 1980.It also contains a very good amount of pictures of rigs and has a photo of Engine Company 308's quarters in Queens with a mural on the door that any buff or person will want to see.

5. **Firegroundphotos.net**

   Containing photos of apparatus from all five boroughs and firehouses from all five boroughs, it is a great visit on the World Wide Web. It also contains photos from the Northeast and the Chicago area.

6. **Eagleemblems.com**

   This website sells patches, shirts, and hats, not just from New York, but from all over the northeast and country. It also carries "Workshirts" or "Jobshirts", which are what the firefighters wear when they are on duty for sale to the public!

7. **Firecollector.com**

This website actually sells old fire helmets, possibly for reuse, but they also have a very very extensive collection of patches from New York City, including old patches no longer used!

8. **Fireapparatusjournal.com**

The official website of the journal of the same name, with a fair amount of good content from their magazines, it is a good spot for buffs to visit.

9. **FDNYTRUCKS.com**

This site, run by Hackensack, New Jersey firefighter Michael Martinelli, contains photos of every fire engine currently used by the FDNY and other old ones. It is constantly being updated, and it also contains photos of rigs from the New York Metro Area. The best source in following the FDNY's rigs!

10. **chiefsaide.tripod.com**

Called "an FDNY beginner's guide", it is the perfect place for upstart buffs or old buffs to learn about the FDNY. It contains information about the chain of command, the serial numbers of apparatus, information about S.O.C., The Fire Patrol (a separate agency run by the New York Board of Fire Underwriters), and a map of firehouses in Manhattan up to 105th Street. It lives up to its' URL!

11. **fdnyphoto.com**

Another site run by a professional photographer, a Mr. Steve Spak, that actually is related to Don Van Holt's site. This features many photos of apparatus and major fires, and has followed the World Trade Center incident scrupulously from September 11th all the way up to ceremony on May 30th. This site also features a special section devoted to some older and more interesting firehouse, including some that we've talked about, like the Jay Street firehouse and the house on Lafayette Street in Manhattan. Steve Spak also did work on the late Captain Brian Hickey's documentary "Brothers in Battle". This site is a great visit for all 'da buffs!

12. **http://members.aol.com/fd347/index.htm**

This website, run by FDNY Fire Dispatcher Frank Raffa, has a first-hand account of what it was like to be a dispatcher during the September 11th terrorist attack, and has many stories of fires over the past decade or so, including a building collapse in downtown Brooklyn on State Street, and other great information, including some colloquial radio terms, like MUNGO (abondoned fire in an oil drum for the purpose of melting copper wire), and the FAST truck (engine or ladder company assigned to respond instantly if a Mayday or a 10-75 goes through).He calls his website the "Little Hole in the Web", and it actually isn't that little! He also keeps a list of all the members recovered since September 11th, and has a list of the appartus lost on September 11th. He also has a program on the site that locates boxes (type up 4 numbers, and it will locate where that box is). Go visit his "Little Hole in the Web", it's not as little as he thinks it is!

13. **fdnyengine6.org,   ladder18fdny.com,   fdnyres1cue.com, fdnyrescue2.com,   fdnyrescue3.com,   rescue4.com, rescue5fdny.com, squad288.com, dragonfighters.com, elbarriosbravest.com, eng202lad101.tripod.com, fdnymarine 6.com,(just to name a few).**

All of these are the official company pages of Engine 6, Ladder 18, Rescues 1-5, Squad 288, Engine 9/Ladder 6 in Chinatown, Engine 53/Ladder 43 in Lower Harlem, and Engine 202/Ladder 101/Battalion 32 in the Red Hook section of Brooklyn, and Marine Company 6 in Brooklyn (at the Navy Yard). just to name a couple of companies who have their own websites. There are others I'm sure, but I can't think of them right off the top of my head presently. All of them contain history and some nifty stuff on the pages, and some of them, especially the Rescue pages also carry information about September 11th, as does Engine 6's site. On some websites, you can even purchase company merchandise, like Rescue 1 and 2's sites.

C. Videos and Documentaries

1. "F.D.N.Y.: Brothers in Battle". This documentary provided a comprehensive look at the FDNY in the late 80s/early 90s. There is also some very unique and astounding footage of fire scenes, especially of a building collapse in Brooklyn. It also has good footage of firehouse life, especially at Engine 292/Rescue 4, and of Medal Day in 1990, the first Medal Day after the infamous "Happy Land" social club fire in the Bronx, where 87 people died. As aforementioned, this was made by the late Captain Brian Hickey of Rescue Company 4 and his late brother R.P. Hickey, and is one of the few if not the only documentaries made about firefighters by firefighters. It was an episode of *Investigative Reports* on A&E, but I believe is avaiable for sale to the general public through some websites.

2. "9-11". This documentary was explained earlier with Engine 7/Ladder 1/Battalion 1, but I will say that if one has the heart to watch this completely through, one will be shocked and amazed, and probably will have been grateful for watching it, as I was. I'm not aware if it is for sale to the public yet, but check.

3. "Firemen in the Bronx". This documentary followed firefighters at several Bronx firehouses in 2000, of note, Engine 48/Ladder 56/Division 7, Engine 79/Ladder 37/Battalion 27, and Rescue 3. It also deals a little bit with arson investigation with the Bronx, and how although crime is decreasing, arson continues to increase. It also provides a rare look into firehouse life, and a firefighter actually saving a child! Aired by PBS, it is a top choice for anybody who wants to learn about the FDNY but doesn't have much spare time (it only is 30 minutes).

4.   A Discovery Channel Program on Rescue Company 3. This documentary aired on March 8th, just days before "9-11" aired, and was a wonderful look at life at Rescue 3 before and after September 11th, and the effects that the deaths of their members had. Check it out!

In addition to these, there are many other FDNY and fire department related documentaries available through Eagleemblems.com and other sites where one can shop for FDNY related things.

Note: All websites seen here, all videos, and all books were used as resources in researching information for this book. My cordial thanks to all the authors, publishers, firefighters (active and retired), producers, directors, cameramen, and webmasters here who devote their time and energy to the field of firefighting and to us buffs! Thank you all!

To contact the author, please send me e-mail directed to jstaten121@aol.com

0-595-24602-8

Printed in the United States
24318LVS00004B/430-432

9 780595 246021